DETAILS OF DINGHY BUILDING

Straight is the line of duty;
Curved is the line of beauty;
Follow the straight line, thou shalt see
The curved line ever follow thee.

                    WILLIAM MACCALL (1812–1888)

The aim of this book is to share knowledge. Every attempt has been made to clarify process, but take heed—these are the workings of a muddled mind. There are many ways to meet a challenge and the following is offered only as one of many routes. It will be a great success if these pages engender new ideas and new methods. In any field you must persevere to achieve your goals.

I would like to thank my wife and children, Sara, Alfie and Grace for allowing me to put so much time into boats.

I would like to thank Dick Wynne of Lodestar Books for the encouragement and time that have brought this book project to fruition.

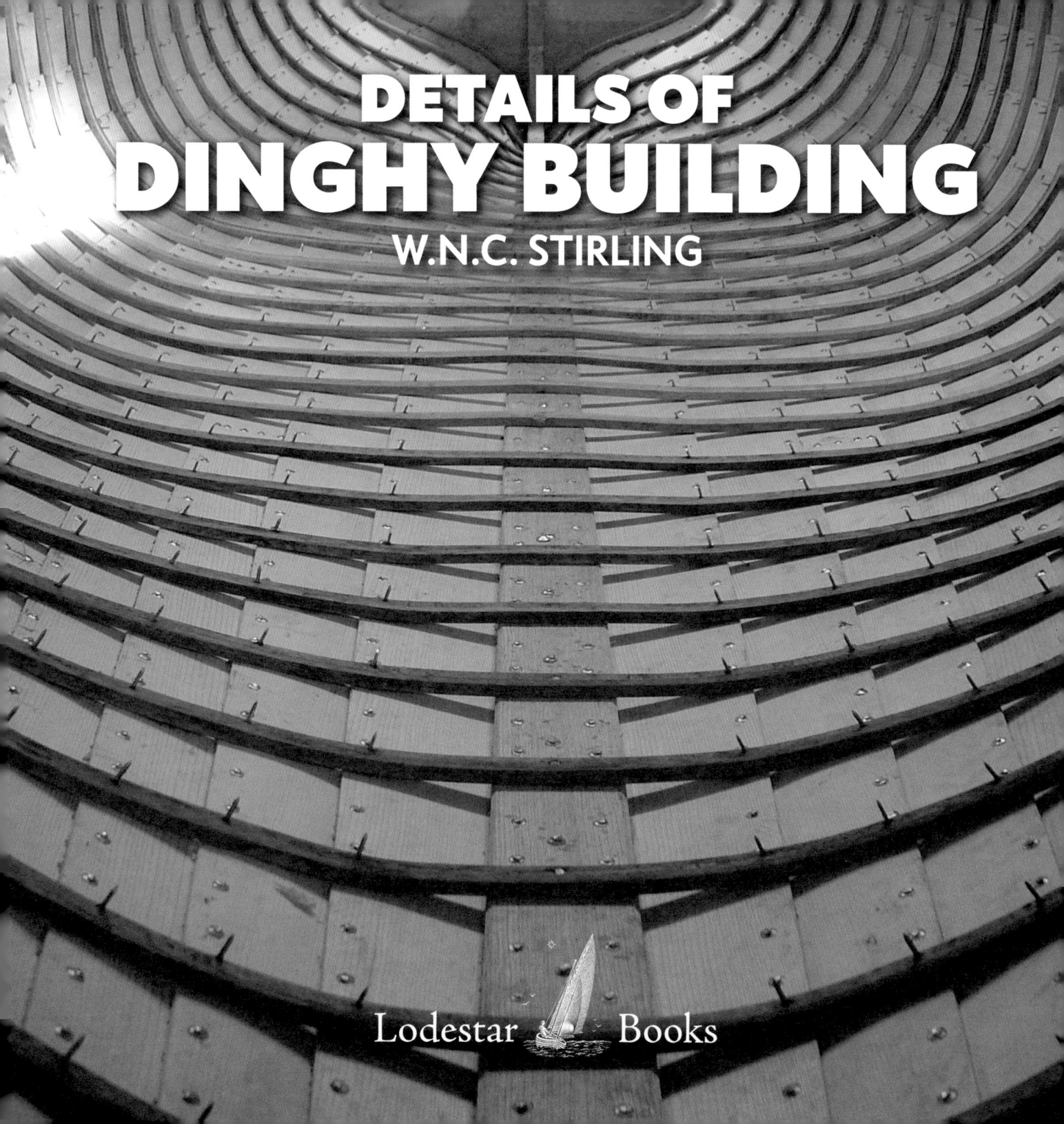

DETAILS OF DINGHY BUILDING
W.N.C. STIRLING

Lodestar Books

Contents

1	Stem assembly	7
2	Transom	11
3	Stern assembly	13
4	Building frame	20
5	Backbone	25
6	Riveting	30
7	Transom bevels	37
8	Rabbet	41
9	Stem and stern bearding	49
10	Stopwaters	52
11	Lining out	55
12	Garboards	58
13	Plank spiling and cutting out	68
14	Planking	75
15	Plank lands	85
16	Bilge runners	90
17	Timbering	92
18	Gunwale and rising	101
19	Thwarts	106

20	Knees	112
21	Rubbing strake and capping rail	119
22	Rowlocks	123
23	Sole boards	125
24	Odds and ends	131
25	Name carving	135
26	Oars	140
27	Waterline	146
28	Rubbing bands	151
29	Sailing dinghy backbone	153
30	Centreboard case	161
31	Centreplate	165
32	Rudder	167
33	Deck beams	172
34	Deck	175
35	Mast step and partners	181
36	Mainsheet horse	184
37	Leather work	187

1   Stem assembly

It is often difficult to find an oak bend with the necessary 'hockey stick' curved grain for a dinghy stem. By joining two pieces together and backing them up with a knee, an equally strong stem assembly can be made from more readily available timber.

Take the templates made on the loft floor, or given in the plans, and try them in different positions on your wood. A little sweep in the grain is good in order to follow the curve of the stem and forefoot piece, and can often be found as the timber comes towards a knot, or at the butt end of a log where the tree came towards the ground.

Make the best use of timber. Come close up to the sap; it may be going away so consider if sap will be removed later in the shaping process. One of our older and now retired shipwrights had himself been apprenticed to an old shipwright, who had himself been apprenticed to men who had worked in the late 19th century Fowey schooner building yards. The line that had been handed down was, 'If I don't see some sap on the edge of that timber boy, I will think you are wasting wood.' Whilst I don't want to see any sap in the boat, as the man who pays for the yard's materials, I fully endorse the sentiment.

Once the faying faces of the joint are flat and square, 'kerf' the nibs with a saw cut. Hopefully after a couple of kerfs the nibs ought to fit with the required fag paper tolerance. Japanese saws are good as they have such a thin blade.

Glue the stem and forefoot piece together. A simple jig as pictured can stop the parts sliding about whilst glueing. We tend to use a polyurethane glue which cures in approximately two hours and is strong enough when one considers that the fastenings will be doing the real work in the future as the ship sails on and the years become decades.

Once the stem and forefoot piece are glued together, glue in the stem knee. The glue will preserve the peace because the stem assembly can be nailed and riveted at leisure and with confidence that it will remain as originally fitted.

In order to fasten, drill the holes from the inside out. The reasoning is that if you wander a little it is easier to accommodate an off centre hole in the wider and plugged face of the stem than on the narrower stem knee.

Some like to clamp a guide stick onto the side of the stem and along the line of the proposed hole, the guide stick protruding say six inches beyond the stem knee. This can be eyed through to keep a parallel gap between the stick and the drill bit in order to help the hole remain central. The guide stick can get in the way a bit.

If it is difficult to find a long enough drill bit, use a bike spoke and flatten the end into a

1.1: Templates and timber

1.2: Selecting a bend for the stem of a sailing dinghy

1.3: Saw kerf for final fit

1.4: A simple jig to hold the stem assembly whilst glueing

point or an arrow head. A selection of reasonable quality bike spokes are generally available outside any good railway station. The bike spoke will be good enough to make a pilot hole which can then be reamed out from either end with the correct drill bit.

For a dinghy, use 10G by 4in and 5in square cut copper nails with 7/16in roves. Extremely long nails are not necessary. As there is a good depth of timber the nails can be counterbored into the face of the stem with a 10mm spade bit and the holes plugged. You may need to stick a small dowel into the hole prior to counterboring with the spade bit because the bit can wobble around if the point is not captive. Another option for counterboring is a Forstner bit. In order to keep this steady, drill through a ¼in piece of scrap timber and hold it over the proposed hole site as a guide. If you can't hold the guide steady, tack it on with a couple of panel pins.

1.5: Stem knee from a bend

1.6: Stem near a knot knee

1.7: Stem knee glued in

1.8: Using a guide to drill the stem assembly fastenings

Plug the counterbores with timber (paying attention to the grain) so that when the brass stem band is fastened on at the end of the job one can get a good hold with the stem band screws in the event of a fastening landing on a plug.

Once complete, the stem assembly can be put to one side until the other backbone members are prepared.

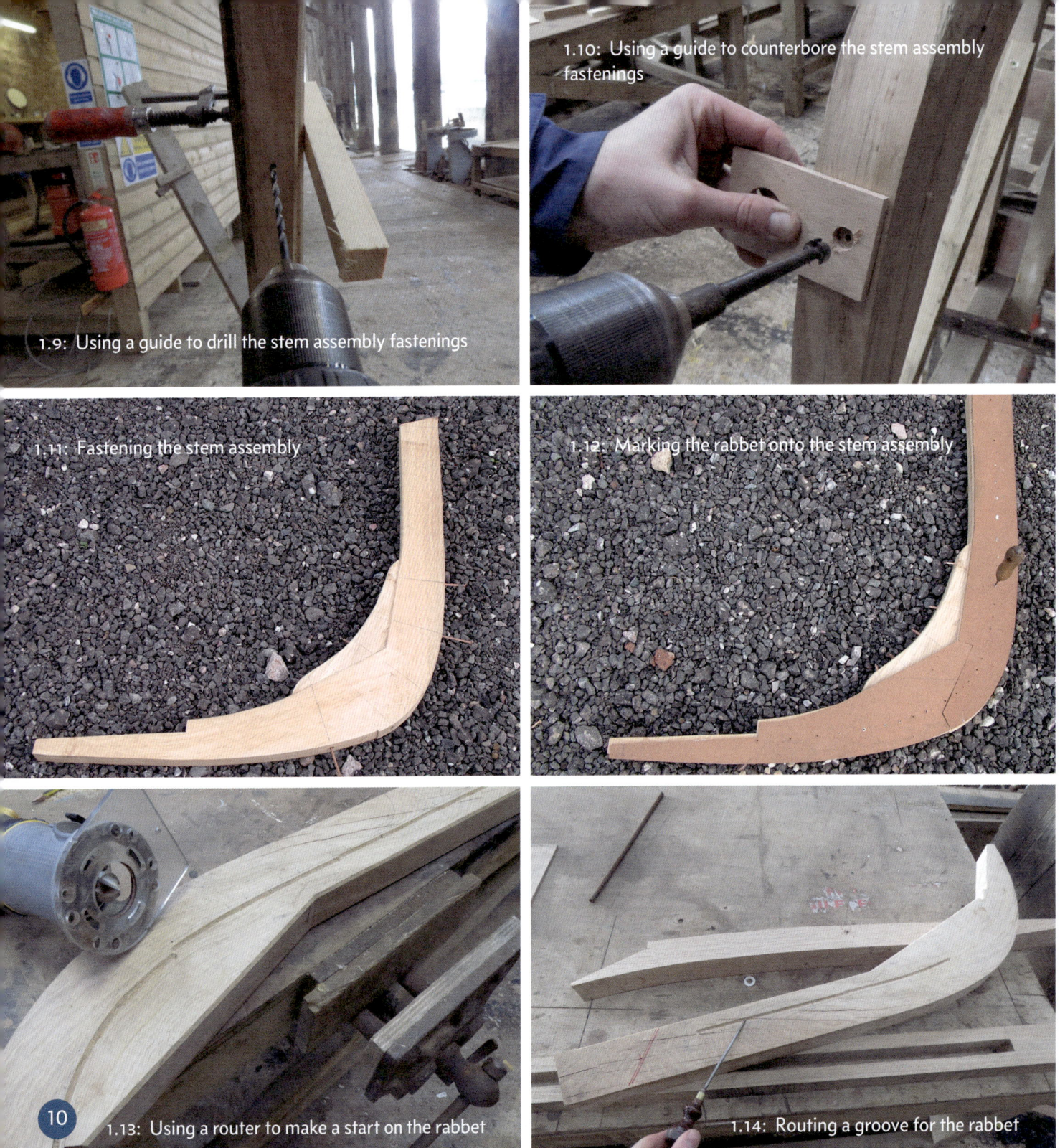

2 Transom

As an old bargemaster advised me, 'I'd like you to build a punt for me; a steady boat, not tender, and mind you well that transom will need to be pretty.'

I later saw the punt on his ship's side deck with the transom facing aft and the old man at the helm. 'Thank you,' the bargemaster said, 'I spend a good deal of time looking at that transom.'

A D-shaped transom is easier to plank and increases buoyancy aft but it is nothing to look at.

Unless a single piece of timber can be found for the transom, two or three boards will need to be jointed together with a groove and fillet. Choose the boards with a view to the grain as jointed wood with carefully selected grain can seem like a single piece.

Allow at least an inch of extra timber around the transom template, which represents the outboard face of the transom. As the boat gets wider towards the middle, the inboard face will be larger than the outboard.

Joint the transom boards together with a loose tongue. Bear in mind that the joints do not want to be close to the top or bottom of the transom. It is best to glue here with epoxy because the joints are not mechanically fastened and it would be a bore if the transom unzipped in the future.

Draw a centreline on the jointed timber at right angles to one of the joints. This is useful because at the end of the job when you are carving your beloved's name into the transom, to be lettered in gold leaf, if the joints are parallel with the water line they can be used as a datum for the carving measurements.

Use a half template for the transom because then it is certain to be the same on both sides.

Once the wood for the transom has been glued up and cleaned off, place the transom template on the board, line it up with the centreline and draw a firm line round it. This line will be the shape of the aft face of the transom.

Set the jigsaw bevelling bed to 45 degrees and cut around the line of the transom template. Make sure that the jigsaw cut direction is making the transom bigger on the inside. This will ensure that there is enough timber for bevelling off later.

Cut the top off the transom with the jigsaw set square. Once the transom is cut to shape mark the plank positions on the aft face and put it to one side for a moment.

2.1: Straight and square

2.2: Fillet and groove joints

2.3: Marking out

2.4: Cutting out the transom with an angled jigsaw

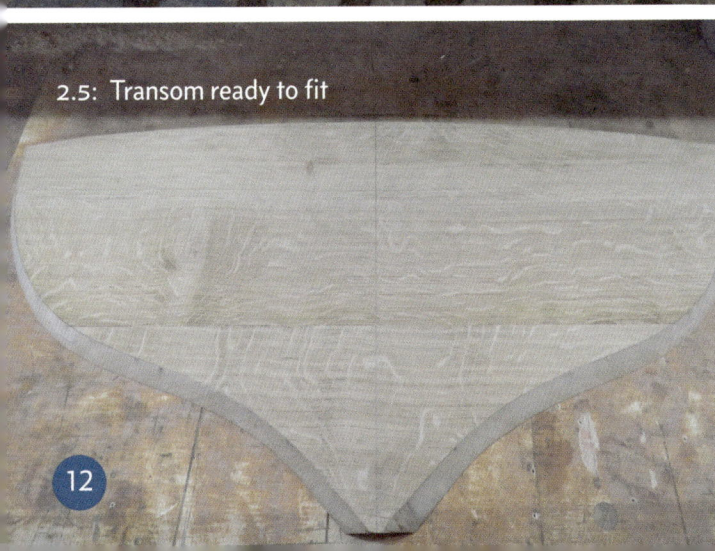
2.5: Transom ready to fit

2.6: Three boards of carefully selected grain

3   Stern assembly

Cut the skeg and the sternpost out using the templates as patterns. It is important to get the angle of the sternpost heel correct because this angle will dictate the rake of your transom.

Mark the mortise onto the skeg using the thirds rule of thumb (⅓ wall: ⅓ mortise: ⅓ wall). This will also inform the width of the tenon on the sternpost, which is not marked to the thirds rule because the siding of the sternpost is greater than that of the skeg.

Once the sternpost tenon is cut, take away its sharp edges as, unless you have managed to be admirably precise in the dark corners of your mortise cutting, the sharp corners might just keep the tenon from going perfectly home.

In order to speed up the mortise cutting, use a drill bit a little smaller than the mortise to mitigate irregular drilling. Drill several holes and clean out with a chisel.

Having cut the tenon on the sternpost, dry fit it into the skeg mortise. If the walls of the mortise and the tenon are square the sternpost will stick up straight. If not the sternpost may list to port or starboard. At best you will be in command of a twisted ship; at worst she won't track straight when you are under easy oar. Once sure that the assembly is straight remove the sternpost and lay it aside.

Steam the after end of the hog and clamp it onto the skeg. When the hog has cooled for a few hours remove it and lay it aside as well.

Glue the stern post into the skeg and once the glue has cured put a 12G × 1in bronze gripfast nail through the tenon.

Cut a slot in the hog so that it can fit around the sternpost. The slot will be the width of the sternpost and ½in longer than the depth of the sternpost fore and aft. Cut the forward end of the slot with a chisel at a bevel equal to the angle between skeg and sternpost.

Clamp the hog to the skeg as a dry fit and set it back with a tap from the hammer so that it fits against the sternpost. Once permission to proceed has been issued by the quality controller, glue the hog onto the skeg, holding the skeg in a vice with the bottom edge of the sternpost flush with the top of the vice, so that the two sides of the cut-out in the hog are held up (having no support they are inclined to sag down a little).

Once the glue has cured, cut the hog off flush with the aft side of the sternpost. Later on, the transom will cover the end grain of the hog.

The sternpost knee has an obtuse angle and can usually be found with adequate grain as a single piece if the board has some sweep to the grain, or there is a large knot which distorts the grain. Be sure that the grain is not short through

3.1: Selecting timber close to the sap

3.2: Shaping a sailing dinghy skeg

3.3: Sternpost, skeg and stern knee

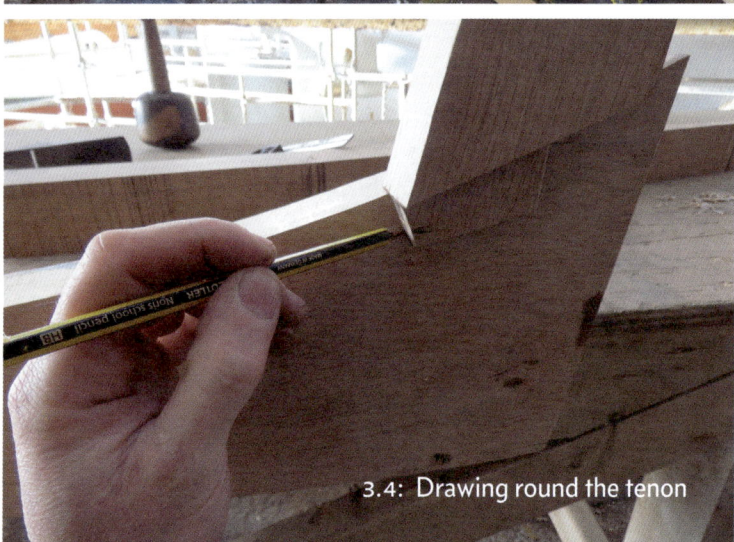
3.4: Drawing round the tenon

the board if the knee comes very close to a knot. Fit and glue the sternpost knee to the stern assembly. This is not structural gluing but will assist in fastening and will also keep water out of the joint. Once it gets damp in the joint it will rarely dry out and long term that will promote softness in the timber, as one often finds where two surfaces mate. It is worth bearing in mind that the glue can stain the wood. To keep cleanup to a minimum, keep the use of glue to a minimum (unless, in company with many boat builders, you are a shareholder in the glue firm—in which case use liberally and lose the lid).

Before fastening, fit the transom. Mark a centre point on the top of the sternpost, aft end of the skeg, and a centreline on the forward face and aft face of the transom. Cut a bevel on the bottom of the transom equal to the bevel between keel and sternpost. Line up the centreline on the sternpost with the centreline on the transom.

3.5: Marking out the mortise

3.6: Clearing out the tenon with a drill

3.7: Cleaning out the tenon with a chisel

3.8: Taking the sharp edges off the tenon

Clamp the transom onto the sternpost, lining up the centre marks. If the angle at the bottom of the transom needs adjusting, saw kerf the joint and tap the transom down.

Glue the transom onto the aft face of the stern post and then fasten the stern assembly together. Lay out your fastenings thoughtfully; those on the transom need to avoid the tongue-and-groove areas but do want to be within two inches of the edge of the joints to prevent any board curling in the future. Bear in mind that the sternpost ring bolt will act as one copper nail.

Be careful when drilling out for the stern knee fastenings that go down through the skeg. On one regrettably memorable occasion I, as tutor of a dinghy building course, had gathered the students about me in order to demonstrate how to drill through the stern post knee and skeg. Once the drum roll had finished and final phone texts had been sent, full concentration was upon

3.9: Steaming the hog

3.10: Gluing the sternpost into the mortise

3.11: Taking the bevel for the hog cut out

3.12: Dry fitting the hog

me. I proceeded to perform, the drill emerging out of the side of the skeg, a long way from the centre of its base. There have been many dinghies; it hadn't happened before nor has it happened since. It was reasonably embarrassing.

The hole is too long through the lowest part of the transom for a nail and rivet so drive a 10G gripfast nail through the lowest part of the transom and into the sternpost. The hole is also too long through the after part of the sternpost knee where it sits on the hog. Drive a 10G gripfast nail through the stern post knee and into the hog and skeg. As with the stem assembly, the sternpost assembly fastenings are 10G square cut copper boat nails and the roves $7/16$in. Plan the fastenings using a ringbolt in place of one rivet.

3.13: Preparing to glue the hog onto the skeg

3.14: Glueing the hog on

3.15: Cutting the excess off the back of the hog

3.16: Lining up the sternpost and transom centrelines

3 Stern assembly

3.17: Saw kerfing the bottom of the transom

3.18: Glueing the transom onto the stern assembly

3.19: Sternpost knee

3.20: Scribing in the foot of the stern post knee

3.21: Glueing the stern post knee

3.22: Fastening the stern assembly

3.23: Gripfast nail at heel of transom

3.24: Nail in the stern knee

3 Stern assembly

4 Building frame

Lofting is a well-documented process that is not addressed in this volume. Hopefully your kind designer has supplied mould patterns with the run of the planking marked out so that you don't have to spend any time on your knees confusing buttocks with stations and wondering why nothing seems to match up as precisely as it should.

Certainly lofting is a drawn out process; precision is required in order to get the correct shapes for the moulds. Lofting, whilst the foundation of the build, is only one small part of the job. Do it correctly and accurately but don't lose construction time fiddling around with lines that do not matter. Ultimately the loft floor needs to supply the shape of the backbone templates and the building moulds.

Mycology: The loft floor shouldn't be down long enough for fungi to develop. If the excessive spread of mould is detected, it is time to think, 'Been down so long it feels like up to me'.

The Barnett Method of transferring shapes from the loft floor to templates can be used for boats of any size. It is simple, quick and gives a fair line straight away. Cut several long oblongs of thin pattern plywood. The pattern ply we tend to use is 3.6mm red-faced ply. These oblongs of approximately 18in by 2in are called 'tad-nabs'. A corner of the tad-nab touches the line to be transferred whilst the main body of the tad-nab is on the outboard side of the line. Screw the tad-nab down to the loft floor with two little Pozidriv screws so that it cannot pivot. Keep these screws as far from the line as possible.

Slip a piece of pattern ply under all of the tad-nabs and put a couple of fastenings in it so that it can't move. Choose a suitable batten and bend it into position so that it touches all of the tad-nabs. Draw round the outside of the batten.

If the lofted lines are to the outside of the planking, reduction of the lines to the inside can be done at this point by using a batten that is the thickness of the planking and by drawing around the inside of the batten; this method of planking reduction can only be used up to a planking thickness of ¾in.

The mould patterns are only half-moulds. They are 'butterflied' over a centreline in order to give the same shape to both side of the boat. Either cut the moulds from ¾in plywood or build them from cheap pine. The cheap pine moulds do last longer than plywood moulds.

At this point, if the run of the planking is marked on the mould patterns supplied by the designer, transfer these onto the mould. Mark them into the mould edge with a saw cut. As one old shipwright advised me with wonderful diction: 'Saw cut him, saw cut him boy! 'Tis goin' to

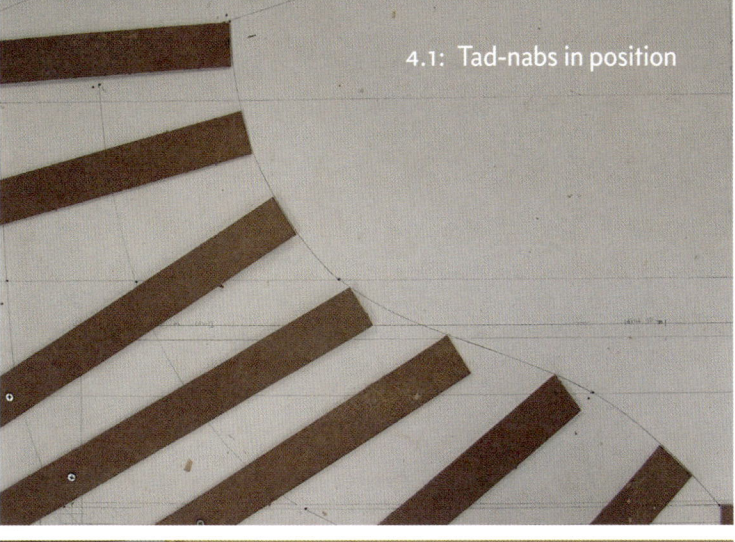
4.1: Tad-nabs in position

4.2: Slipping the hardboard under the tad-nabs

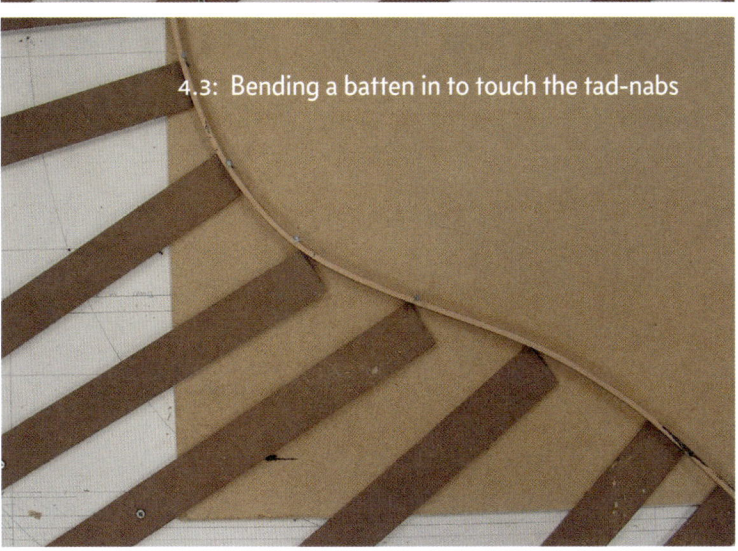
4.3: Bending a batten in to touch the tad-nabs

4.4: Line transferred to template

4 Building frame

last more longer than a pencil line you see!' If the planking marks are not supplied with mould patterns the run of the planking will need to be lined out when the rabbet has been cut.

The strong-back must be the length of the dinghy and it must be straight! A piece of tanalised pine 6in by 3in seems to work well. The strong-back is set up on two trestles. The tops of the two trestles must be in the same horizontal plane. Fasten the strong-back to the trestles with a pair of 2in by 2in blocks on each trestle. The midships mould is the first to be set up. Measure aft from the front of the strong-back the half-length of the dinghy minus the fore and aft depth of the stem at sheer. This is the position of the centre of the mid-ships mould. Mark a line square across the strong-back and square down each side. Note this line as mid-ships. Draw a second line parallel to the first across the top of the strong-back and half the thickness of the building mould away

4.5: Rowing dinghy pine moulds

4.6: Rowing dinghy mould bracing to trestle

4.7: Planking marks kerfed into the mould

from the mid-ships line. This can be forward or aft of the mid-ships line. This second line will be the mark that the mould lines up with.

Square the second line down the sides of the strong-back and set up a length of 2in by 2in cheap pine on each side of the strong-back and lined up with the mark. They should be vertical and square to the strong-back. Screw these vertical or upstanding timbers to the side of the strong-back with two screws.

Attach the mould to the pine upstands. The thwartships centreline of the mould must be on the fore-and-aft centreline of the strong-back. Mark the end-of-dinghy position on the strong-back. Later you can use a set square from this line to find the fore and aft position of the top aft face of the transom in relation to the building frame.

Returning to the mid-ships mould, measure fore and aft to find the positions of the intermediate moulds. Once all of the moulds are in place, it it is useful to screw legs onto the building frame and down to the floor so that the frame doesn't twist and wobble when bending the planks around it later. Quite a neat way of fixing the legs is to line the trestles up with a forward and an after mould. The legs prop down from the mould onto the trestle. This allows best access between the moulds when riveting planks later.

Check the measurement between the end-of-dinghy mark and the forward end of the strong-back. This should be the length of the dinghy less the fore-and-aft depth of the stem. It is worth being precise with this. Check that the moulds are 'plumbed and horned'. This is a colourful way of saying set up straight. Plumbing and horning can be done with a spirit level. The spirit level used vertically against a mould will show you if the moulds are vertical, and if you put the level along the flat 'head' of the mould (the part nearest the floor) the mould can be checked for level athwartships. It is important that the moulds are all level, and level relative to each other, because the sheer line is marked on the moulds; the sheer line will only be a fair line if the moulds are all in their correct locations and all thoroughly plumbed and horned.

5 Backbone

The backbone assembly is made of three sections: the stem assembly, the keel, and the stern assembly.

The stern assembly is the first to be attached to the building frame. The hog will already be attached to the transom assembly and is located in the centre-line notches cut out of the building moulds. The top of the transom is lined up with the 'end-of-boat' mark on the strong-back.

Fasten the transom assembly to the strong-back with two pieces of 2in by 2in pine, screwed onto both sides of the strong-back and the inboard face of the transom on both sides of the sternpost. Make sure that the fastenings through the pieces of pine and into the transom are level with each other. At the end of the job the holes left behind in the transom will be plugged and one doesn't want them to look like a clown's glasses with eye balls on springs at every different angle.

Once the transom is attached to the building frame, fasten the hog to each mould with a small cleat, fastened to the building moulds with two screws and to the hog with a single screw. The skeg is also already attached to the transom assembly, with the scarph between skeg and keel cut by prior arrangement on the bench, before the skeg was fastened to the transom assembly.

The keel is a straight piece of timber. Clamp the keel alongside the skeg and draw round the skeg scarph onto the side of the keel. Take the keel back to the bench and cut out the scarph, removing the pencil line and no more.

Once the scarph fits, possibly having had a final saw kerf, glue the keel onto the hog. Before the glue sets, make sure that the keel is straight on the hog and is in line with the skeg. A bent backbone at this stage will haunt the rest of the job.

It is sometimes difficult to sight down the keel at the time of glueing due to the clamps. One means of ensuring straightness is to clamp a straightedge alongside the keel and skeg. A piece of timber would be fine; we tend to use a piece of rectangular section aluminium.

Two components of the backbone assembly are now together, with the forward end of the keel and hog left square and overhanging the forward mould. The stem assembly now remains to be attached to the forward end of the building strong-back and jointed to the forward end of the keel. The scarph on the stem assembly will have already been cut as for the skeg: on the bench.

Note the position of the sheer at the stem in relation to the strong-back. Hold the stem on the forward end of the strong-back by pushing on the stem's forward face with your knee, making sure that the sheer mark is in the correct position.

This temporary positioning by genu-clamp should be to one side of the centreline so that the

5.1: Stern assembly fitted to building frame

5.2: Marking out the skeg to keel scarph

stem assembly at the scarph end can be clamped onto the side of the hog and keel.

Using a spirit level against the forward edge of the stem ensure there is a little rake aft. Despite the apparent plumb dinghy stem on paper, it is in practice raked a little aft. If fitted exactly plumb it will appear to be raked aft at stemhead and it simply isn't fashionable to go to sea in a miniature Dreadnought in the current political climate.

Once the rake of the stem is correct, tracing the shape of the stem assembly scarph, pencil mark the hog and keel. Cut the keel and hog part of the scarph in position. This is always awkward.

Glue the stem assembly onto the keel, being sure to sight down the keel to check everything is in line. The use of polyurethane glue for backbone assembly is permissible. Not only does it create a stronger and more homogenous backbone, it also greatly assists the boat builder in their pursuit of the perfectly fitted joint.

Once the glue has cured fasten at leisure and with the happy assurance that the previously excellent dry fit will not become a joint saddled with excuses whilst having a large copper nail driven through it.

The fastenings in the keel should be carefully laid out because they will dictate the planking and timber fastenings. Start in the nib of the keel-to-skeg scarph. Drill for a fastening every six inches forward of this until you reach the stem assembly. Later the steam-bent timber will cross the keel half way between the hog-to-keel fastenings. In other words the distance between any hog-to-keel fastening and the centre of a timber will be three inches.

This pattern may become dishevelled at the stem-to-keel scarph; of greater importance than a pretty pattern is a well fastened joint. There will be perhaps three fastenings through the stem-to-keel scarph, and these go where they need to go with no regard for the spacings. Having fastened

5.3: Marking out the skeg to keel scarph

5.4: Dry fitting the skeg to keel scarph

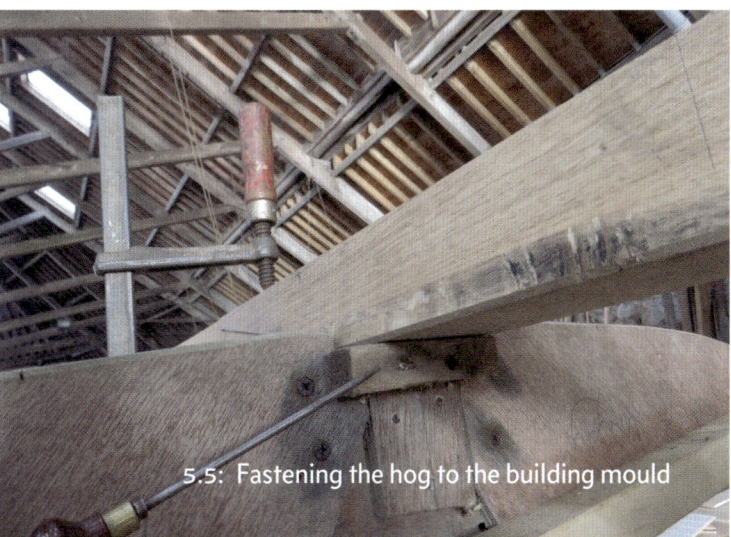
5.5: Fastening the hog to the building mould

5.6: Stem assembly to keel and hog scarph

forward of the keel-to-skeg scarph, continue the six-inch spacing aft of the keel-to-stem scarph. At some point you will arrive at the sternpost knee.

Should this be a sailing dinghy the rivets will be left out entirely in way of the centre-case slot. This is because the centre-case itself has to be fitted inside the dinghy and a row of limpet heads inside will prevent a good fit. Be sure to measure carefully and continue the six-inch spacing so that the first rivet forward of the centre-case slot is a multiple of six inches forward of the last rivet aft of the slot.

5.7: Using the knee clamp to set up

5.8: Glueing the stem

5.9: Glueing the stem asssembly to the keel

5.10: Fastening pattern in the stem assembly to keel scarph

5.11: Pine clamp to connect the stem head to the strong back

5.12: Fastening the keel to the hog

5.13: Fastenings as necessary in the keel to stem assembly scarph

5.14: Ready to rabbet

5 Backbone

6   Riveting

A clinker dinghy is stitched together with over a thousand copper rivets; these are made up from square cut copper boat nails and round, slightly conical copper washers called roves. The backbone rivets are 10G with a ⁷⁄₁₆ in rove; the drill size for a 10G nail is 4mm. The planking is fastened together with 13G nails; the drill size for a 13G nail is 2.5mm or 3mm if you feel 2.5 is a bit tight. The gripfast nails in the hood ends are 12G by 1in which take a 3mm clearance and a 2.5mm pilot hole.

The riveting process is as follows: Drill a hole, countersink the outboard side of the hole and poke the nail through. Hold a heavy flat weight (a dolly—which might have once been the head of a 7lb hammer) on the nail head and drive a rove onto the nail with a rove punch (piece of metal with a hole drilled in it and countersunk). Cut off the excess copper nail with a pair of snips, leaving the width of the nail proud of the rove. Still backing up with the heavy weight, rivet the copper over the rove with a small ball pein hammer. Start with a few taps from the flat side of the hammer, continue to tighten over going around the nail head with the rounded side of the hammer and finish off with a few taps to neaten up from the flat side of the hammer. Don't bludgeon it to death as the nail will cripple inside the hole. Just tap, tap, tap away until it all looks neat and tight. The power of the rivet to pull timber together is wonderful.

Neat fastenings are an essential and a time consuming part of any boatbuilding job. Fastenings are particularly evident on a dinghy hull because they remain on the surface of the timber. Planning for the fastenings starts right at the beginning of the job. One has to set off in the right direction in order to ensure that once built the dinghy's fastenings present a uniform visual impression. The positioning of the first fastenings that go in the boat (the keel to hog fastenings) affects the planking fastenings.

Start at the keel to hog scarph and drill a hole from the outside through keel and hog every six inches. Work forward until you arrive at the keel to forefoot scarph. Here the spacing may change for one or two nails to suit the scarph. The spacing of the oak ribs will be six inches from centre to centre. Each rib will be fastened centrally between two keel-to-hog fastenings. This configuration will dictate the planking fastenings.

The planking lands have two 1in by 13G fastenings between adjacent ribs and thus the planking is fastened every two inches (once the ribs are in). Before the ribs go in the planking fastenings are in sets of two, two inches apart with a gap of four inches until the next set. Once

6.1: Riveting tools

6.2: 3/8-inch chock to get the garboard to hog fastenings in a neat line

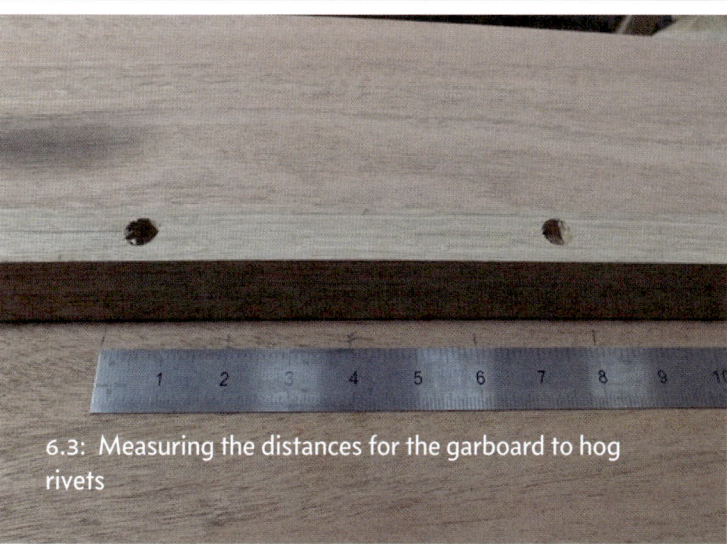

6.3: Measuring the distances for the garboard to hog rivets

6.4: Garboard-to-hog nails either side of the centreline fastening

the garboards are fitted run a ⅜in chock of wood along the side of the keel with a pencil mark to get the fastenings through the garboard and hog in an even line. The garboard fastenings will be one inch either side of each keel to hog fastening. This will give a gap of two inches between the fastenings in each set and four between each set. Mirror this on the other side of the keel. Don't blindly rely on looking at the tape measure, check it visually by looking at both sides of the keel at once, because one wants the land fastenings to be the same on both sides.

These sets of two nails, fastening the planking together, have to run at right angles from the keel up to the gunwale. This is difficult because it is further round the gunwale than along the keel so the spacing will slightly change, especially towards the bow where the difference between keel and gunwale is greatest. Midships the lines of nails will remain parallel.

6.5: Changing from copper nails to gripfast nails on the forefoot

In order to mark the fastening positions onto the planking as the hull is planked, first mark the half-width of the plank landing so that the fastenings are in the middle of the landing. Cut a little piece of timber with a notch half the width of the landing. The landing should be ¾in which is equal to twice the thickness of the planking and therefore the notch will be ⅜in long). On the outside of the boat, push the notch against the lower edge of the planking and mark along the face of the plank in the middle of the land. This is where the nails will be drilled. Use a large builder's set square. Hold it parallel with the keel (level in all directions) and on a garboard fastening nail head. Stand in line with the edge to avoid parallax error. With the other hand, pencil mark the plank landing to be fastened. This gets more tricky as the planking goes on because the distance between square edge and plank landing increases, so it has to be done by eyeing through the square and ensuring that

6.6: Notched piece of wood half the land thickness to ensure fastening are in neat line and middle of land

6.7: Marking for land fastenings midships

6.8: Marking for land fastenings midships

the nails fitted in previous planks line up with the edge of the square—a job for a steady hand.

They tell me that the dinghy planker who unerringly spiles the perfect plank only requires one clamp to secure the board to the boat, and that this single lonely clamp remains on the work bench. I seem to need one every eighteen inches because if the two planks are not clamped tightly together when drilling the fastening holes, swarf from the drill lodges between the two planks. If the planking timber is very hard this swarf will hold the two planks apart, foiling the required fag paper fit, or if the planking is softer the swarf will be crushed into the planking between the lands and cause a little permanent damage to the mating faces. Once the nails have been tapped into place the clamps can be removed (and hidden, one left on the bench).

It sometimes happens that there is an awkward rove which refuses to stay on the nail when

6.9: Marking for land fastenings at bow (beginning of planking)

6.11: Marking for land fastenings at stern

6.10: Marking for land fastenings at bow (end of planking)

trying to rivet up. Hold the rove on with a spare hacksaw blade, allowing the nail to poke through the hole in the end of the blade. Rivet a little until the rove stays put. Remove the hacksaw blade and tighten the rivet up.

The small ball pein hammer can leave black marks on both the planking and the timbers if it slips off when riveting. A piece of 3mm pattern ply with a one-inch hole bored through it can be used as a 'salvador' in order to prevent marks around the rove. The salvador will eventually fall to pieces but it is easy enough to make a replacement.

The planking fastenings can be riveted solo. It is a slightly different process to the method above: The boat will be upside down for planking. Having tapped the nail into place, balance the rove in the rove punch countersink and hold it firmly against the nail point. With the flat face of the small ball pein hammer tap the nail head with reasonable

6.12: Using the salvador

6.13: Dolly with an 8mm bolt for countersunk riveting

but not excessive force. This will jump the rove onto the nail. Remove the rove punch and clip the excess nail off. With one hand hold the dolly on the nail head and leaning under the boat rivet the nail. When the boat is the right way up and all the oak timber nails have been fitted the majority can also be riveted solo – the extent depends on arm length. One has the rest of the lower body (hip/thigh) to help back up the dolly as well.

The lower timber fastenings and the garboard wedge fastenings are a two person job. One poor soul will have to lie underneath the boat and hold the dolly against the fastening head whilst the other rivets from inside. A quick double tap at the end of riveting tells the person underneath that the rivet is complete. The person above then says something along the lines, 'Two forward and one up' in order to direct the person underneath to the next nail. Make sure that the person underneath understands the quality control requirements and

6.14: Short nail and hacksaw blade technique

6.15: Uniform fastenings at the end of the job

can firmly hold the dolly against the nail head. Frequent errors are dents in the planking from the edge of the dolly and nails that are not set flush which need to be tightened up. At the end of riveting, a tightened nail is never as neat as a nail set flush first time. For the backbone fastenings which are plugged over we have a hammer head with an 8mm bolt tapped into it. This spike allows weight to be applied against the nail head when it is countersunk.

You can tell when a nail is backed up properly by the sound that it makes: A properly backed up nail will make a sharp 'tack' sound. A nail that is not properly backed up will make a duller 'thud'.

7 Transom bevels

The correct bevel can be put on the transom using three battens and the batten hopping method. Start at the garboard with a batten tacked on the planking marks but let fly over the transom. It must be tacked to at least two moulds. Put a second and third batten in position at the marks for planks two and three.

Bend the first batten gently down until it touches the transom at the garboard mark. It will be touching on the inboard face of the transom. Begin to take timber off the inside edge of the transom, repeatedly gently pulling the batten down to check the bevel progress.

You can use an angle grinder with a sanding disc on to remove the bulk of the wood. We call this an electric chisel; be cautious. For fine tuning use a spoke shave to work the transom edge down until the batten touches right across the transom edge at the selected plank mark.

Be gentle with the batten in order to be sure that it is telling you the truth: it is often possible to force a batten but it will be distorted in the process; the bevel will be wrong and you won't achieve the desired 'fag paper fit'. Once the batten touches at the inboard face, the outboard face and neatly in between, the bevel is correct.

When the top edge of the garboard is correct, move that batten to the marks for plank number four. Work the bevel round the transom. When the bevel is correct at plank two move the batten to plank five and so on. This is batten hopping and it ensures continuity of the bevel up the transom.

The shape is maintained by preserving the pencil line of the transom template on the aft face. Judgement is needed to fair the bevel between the plank marks.

Sometimes a block plane is easier to use than a spoke shave for the sheer plank transom bevel, because this is right across the end grain and a bit of weight behind the tool helps to stop it chattering. To accurately cut the bevel for the garboard between the top edge of the garboard and the rabbet see the section on cutting the rabbet.

7.1: Using batten to indicate the bevel

7.2: The batten shows that timber needs to be taken off the inside of the transom

7.3: The batten shows that timber needs to be taken off the inside of the transom

7.4: Electric chisel

7.5: Flat bottomed spoke shave

7.6: Hopping the battens to come round the turn of the bilge

7.7: Fine tuning the angle by removing small shavings of timber

7.8: Almost there, still a little off the inside

7 Transom bevels

7.9: Fag paper fit

8   Rabbet

To my mind the rabbet is the hardest part of the boat as one has to think in three dimensions while mentally accommodating twist. It is regrettable that this challenge comes at the beginning of the build, although a positive aspect is that once the challenge of the rabbet has been overcome the remainder of the boat is within capability.

For some reason we always start the rabbet towards the back of the boat—perhaps warming up towards the stem forefoot, which is the Cape Horn of the job.

The transom bevels are already complete but there will need to be some work done between the upper edge of the garboard (where the garboard and plank two overlap on the transom) and the rabbet where the garboard meets the skeg.

Starting at the midships mould and facing aft work the hog down to the correct bevel. In order to find the correct bevel, use a six-inch ruler at right angles to the keel across each mould to show you how much wood needs to be taken off the hog so that the hog fairs into the mould. At present, take nothing off the hog where it meets the keel.

Sight along and fair in the hog between each pair of moulds. This gently winding taper on the hog must always be flat thwartships. As the hog reaches the transom it becomes strongly bevelled. Take a thin piece of plywood three feet long and roughly cut to the shape of the garboard. Use this to indicate how much wood needs to be bevelled off. This piece of plywood will also show what needs to be done to the transom between the top edge of the garboard mark and the skeg.

At times using a very sharp chisel and scraping can take the final thwartships bumps out. Do be careful not to slip.

In order to mark the outer rabbet, run a piece of wood that is as thick as the planking along the hog, making a pencil mark above it on the side of the keel. The edge of the plank will be square, therefore the rabbet needs to be square. Put the six-inch ruler on the now-bevelled hog and push it up against the keel. The corner of the ruler will touch where the hog meets the keel but the ruler will not touch the pencil line on the side of the keel.

Using a chisel to rough out and then a rabbet plane or a small bull-nose plane with its side firmly held onto the beveled hog, plane the keel until the blade reaches the pencil line. This will only work where the rabbet is straight. Where there is too much curve for the plane use a chisel alone. The strong angle of the hog as it comes towards the transom means that the corresponding cut into the keel becomes increasingly deeper in order to allow the square plank edge to fit up against the keel.

8.1: Marking the rabbet at the transom

8.2: Marking the rabbet at the transom

8.3: Cutting the rabbet at the transom

8.4: Chiselling the hog flat with a winding bevel

Once the aft rabbet is cut and the thin piece of ply has been offered up a final time, you've checked underneath and confirmed that the aft rabbet is fair and square, gather your wits and head for the bow.

Start the stem rabbet at the sheer line. Start with three battens lightly nailed to the midships and forward moulds and just touching the rabbet, one at the sheer, one at plank seven and one at plank six. Let the batten spring off at the rabbet so that you have room to work. For a depth gauge, take a piece of plank wood that is the same depth as the planking and has a square end on it (perhaps 2in long, ½in wide and ⅜in thick).

There is a guide v-groove in the stem already. Push the batten in at the stem and see if the v-groove is in the right direction. Cut a little more out of the back, a little more out of the front, and so on until when you push the batten in it sits neatly against the back rabbet, and when you put

8.5: Chiselling the hog flat with a winding bevel

8.6: Rabbet cut at the transom

8.7: Planing the hog flat with a winding bevel

8.8: A bump across the hog - more to come off

your depth gauge in flush against the back rabbet it is also touching the fore rabbet and the pencil line of the rabbet marked on the side of the stem.

Don't force the battens, let them give you as much information as they can. Once the rabbet is neat between the sheer and plank seven, take that batten off and move it to plank five. Continue the procedure until you get to plank one, the garboard. On the stem you have the rabbet cut down to the garboard mark. Bevel the hog from the midships mould forward until it runs fair off the forward mould. Now cometh the hardest part of the boat.

The rabbet needs to be joined up between the garboard mark on the stem and the forward mould, and there is apparently nothing to guide the angle. Cut a bit of thin ply so that it is roughly the shape of the forward end of the garboard and reaches back halfway to the midships mould. Cut a small v-groove in the missing bit of rabbet.

8.9: Rebate planing the winding bevel into the hog

8.10: Marking the rabbet line with a chock the thickness of the planking

8.11: Marking the rabbet line with a chock the thickness of the planking

8.12: Chiselling the outer rabbet

Cautiously join up the gap, repeatedly bending the mock garboard end into position so that it shows you what to take off. Take off too little and you will probably break the garboard on a hump. Too much and there is a gap inside.

Eventually you will have a groove that is the depth of your planking gauge, is fair on the rabbet line, the inner rabbet line and the bearding line, has a twisting bevel, and is a masterpiece of form and function. When you build the clipper ship *Thermopylae* the rabbet will present no problem because the twist is drawn out over two hundred feet. In a nine-foot dinghy the same amount of twist is compacted into… nine feet.

8.13: Cutting into the inner rabbet line

8.14: Chiselling the outer rabbet down to the inner rabbet line

8.15: Checking the rabbet and hog are at right angles — more to come off

8.16: The rabbet and hog at right angles

8.17: Cleaning the rabbet with a rebate plane

8.18: Checking the depth of the rabbet with a block

8.19: Preparing to fair the stem assembly to keel joint

8.20: The stem assembly to keel joint faired

8.21: Using battens to determine the stem back rabbet

8.23: Using a planking offcut to check the stem rabbet is the correct depth and the back rabbet is at right angles to the rabbet

8.22: Checking stem rabbet angle with batten

8.24: Using battens to determine the stem back rabbet half way down the stem

8.25: Chiselling the outer rabbet

8 Rabbet

8.26: Chiselling the outer rabbet

8.27: Chiselling the inner rabbet

8.28: Chiselling the inner rabbet

8.29: Using thin and cheap plywood to check the forefoot rabbet

8.30: Looking down the rabbet to check it is fair

9 Stem and stern bearding

We built a lovely boat for HMS *Victory*. The design was sent down from the Royal Naval Archives at Greenwich and although plywood was initially requested we managed to persuade them that building to an original specification would be more appropriate. Accordingly, the specification was sent down and Steel's *Shipwrights' Vade Mecum* became a guiding text for the works.

The boat was beautiful and authentic right down to her ochre and linseed oil finish. A venerable shipwright was reported to say, 'Those men have done a good job; she is a well-built boat. Pity they didn't beard the sternpost though, it looks a bit lumpy.'

That is the enduring memory of the *Victory* yawl build—we could have done just that bit better. For those who want to see an example of a heavy sternpost, the yawl is now on display in perpetuity in Portsmouth.

Every detail counts, forever.

Whilst the stem can be bearded at any point, I have found that it is easier to beard it before planking. The bearding starts in a scallop ½in below the bottom edge of the sheer plank. Mark a centre line down the stem. Mark a line on each side of the centreline and parallel with it at a distance of ⅜in from the centreline.

Bear in mind that when the stem has been bearded its face will be ¾in wide and so will be narrower than the keel; as the bearding works along the forefoot piece it will swell out to meet the forward end of the keel. Therefore, allow the two marked lines to swell out on the forefoot piece to meet the full width of the keel.

A teacup can be used to mark the scallops. The scallops are finished with a wide chisel. Put the bevel edge of the chisel against the timber because the chisel point will tend to come up and away from the timber—this gives you more control; if you put the flat of the chisel against the timber it is liable to dive down into the timber, removing more wood than intended, which may cause distress.

The skeg will need to taper in the vertical view from the transom joint to the heel. On a rowing dinghy, it will be 1⅛in at the transom joint and will taper to ¾in at the heel.

The skeg will need to taper in the horizontal view from keel to skeg scarph to heel. It is best to taper the skeg after the garboards have been fitted because there can be some uneven lateral pressure on the backbone when fitting the garboards, which can cause the backbone to marginally twist. This minute flexing can be visually removed when bearding the skeg.

9.1: Marking the bearding onto the stem, in this case once planking is complete

9.2: Bearded after the rabbet has been cut

9.3: Bearded after the rabbet has been cut

9.4: Bearding marked on the skeg

9.5: Bearding on the sternpost before the garboards have been fitted

9 Stem and stern bearding

10 Stopwaters

Essential and easily forgotten. No matter whether you are building a clinker dinghy or a 100-ton schooner, given that all others parts fit properly, dry feet are maintained by a little pine peg. Any joints in the backbone need a small softwood dowel set across the joint which swells up and prevents the ingress of water. The peg is simply called a 'stopwater'.

The stopwater is put in the joint at the bearding line, where the back rabbet meets the fore rabbet. The hole is drilled exactly in the middle of the joint so that each member (perhaps keel and sternpost) has half a hole in it. Initially drill through with a small drill. If the hole appears on the other side more in the keel than the sternpost it can be adjusted when reaming out with the larger drill. The stopwater must not go through a tenon.

In order to make the peg, drill a hole through a piece of steel at least 10mm thick. Cut a straight and square piece of softwood (for example pine, larch, or spruce) fractionally larger than the hole, with straight and relatively tight grain. Roughly plane eight sides on the peg with a block plane. Tap it through the hole in the steel taking care not to drive the hammer down onto the steel as it will take the sharp edge off the hole.

Drive the stopwater into the hole in the rabbet. Make its grain perpendicular to the joint for optimum effect.

10.1: Getting a stopwater hole started in the rabbet

10.2: Drilled through with a small drill that has come out slightly off centre

10.3: Reamed out with a 6mm drill so the hole is centred on the joint

10.4: Hammering a peg through the dowel plate

10.5: Tapping the stopwater into the rabbet

10.6: Tapping the stopwater into the transom to skeg joint

10.7: A stopwater cut flush with a chisel — note its grain direction, perpendicular to the line of the joint

10 Stopwaters

11 Lining out

Some plans come with the run of the planking marked on the mould templates; this saves the dinghy builder another job. Other plans are a simple set of lines, in which case the run of the planking will need to be set out once the moulds have been erected on the strong-back.

Decide how many planks you would like to have on each side. One generally has the same amount on both sides—I was pleasantly surprised to repair a dinghy which had more planks on one side than the other. How bemused the builder must have been when he finished planking one side and came to realize that there was yet another plank to go on the other side.

The moulds can be split up into equal planking widths with a pair of dividers. This works well if the number of planks is increased making the planking narrow. I prefer slightly wider planking and to govern the sweep of the planking. By lining out each plank individually it can be ensured that in areas of tight turn the planks are narrower, and therefore have a lesser angle on the landing bevels.

Cut battens ¼in thick, the width of the landing and eighteen inches longer than the dinghy's length. The sheer line marks will be on the moulds from the loft floor. If you are having a gunwale capping reduce the sheer by ⅜in and tack the sheer batten in place. That is the top edge of the sheer plank. All of the other battens will mark the bottom edge of the planking.

Different areas have different opinions about planking. I had a spate of building dinghies in Plymouth through a broker on the East Coast. Being an East Coast man he liked to see a parallel sheer plank. Those building the dinghies with me were Westcountry men and liked a good tapered sheer. Given that all involved were liberal in outlook there was a minimum of wailing and gnashing of teeth. Ever ready to agree with everybody and nobody at the same time, I like to see a sheer plank that is relatively parallel yet gently tapering fore and aft.

Fix a batten at the lower edge of the sheer, bearing in mind that the sheer will have two rubbing strakes on it which may account for up to 1½in of visual plank reduction. When complete ideally this plank needs to seem bigger than the rest of the planking. Next decide on the garboard. At the stem the planking between the second plank and the plank below the sheer plank wants to be the same size.

It is often the case that the bottom edge of the third plank comes to the waterline. The second plank may be similar to, but a little wider than, the third plank. The bottom edge of the second plank defines the garboard.

11.1: Lining out planking

11.2: Turning the photo upside down

At the transom the planking is arbitrary. The sheer is defined and must be ⅜in below the top of the transom to allow for the capping to sit on top of the sheer plank yet not be vertically proud of the transom. The remainder of the planking at the transom is lined out to suit its shape. The garboard tends to be of a medium width as there is a bit of twist and hollow. Planks two and three are often quite wide as the transom is quite flat in that area. Planks five, six and seven tend to be narrow as there is a lot of curve at their location.

At the midships mould the garboard and second plank will be wide because the boat is flat. Planks three and four will become narrower as the dinghy begins to turn around the bilge. Plank five will be narrower and six and seven become wider as the sides of the dinghy are straightening up.

Having decided upon the marks at stem, midships mould and transom, the battens will indicate where the planking wants to go on the forward and aft mould. The planking wants to look relatively even on the forward mould with no hint of the hump in planks three four and five as the planking comes to the stem.

Put the battens up and look at the boat from every angle, particularly at the bow and with your head upside down; the less agile can take a digital photo and turn the camera upside down. Once she looks sweet and fair make a saw cut above and below each batten. A saw cut lasts longer than a pencil mark. Because the battens are ¾in wide, which is the plank landing width, the saw cut will give the top and the bottom edge of each plank.

12   Garboards

The garboards are the most difficult planks to fit, the trickiest parts being the two feet at each end.

An eight-foot sheet of 3.6mm redwood ply will be too short to make a pattern in one piece: pattern the forward and after ends separately; then join the two patterns towards the middle of the boat. In the old days, to join patterns we used very short screws, which was incredibly fiddly. They lived in a special battered Fisherman's Friend tin. We then graduated to a pop rivet gun, the moment of transition being accompanied by a great feeling of self-satisfied cleverness. In more recent years an apprentice suggested a hot melt glue gun. Certain levels of insolence can be tolerated; in particular when they are unavoidably correct.

In more detail: To fit the forward pattern cut a rough guess at the shape. Clamp it onto the forward and middle moulds, bend it into the rabbet, and either clamp it gently to the stem or tack it into place with a thin wire nail. Mark the shape using a chock of wood as a spacer between the rabbet and your pencil. Mark the upper edge at stem and transom and the widths at moulds. Put a batten through the outer marks and draw a pencil line. Cut to both the chock-marked line and the batten-marked line. Put the pattern back on the boat. It should now be slightly smaller than the finished plank will be, so that it is reasonably fitted to the rabbet and also within the upper edge markings. At this stage don't be too fussy because this is only getting a general shape before the fine pattern making can begin. Do the same aft.

Connect the two parts and put a 'pitching mark' on the keel and on your pattern; a pitching mark is one that indicates where the pattern or plank fits on the boat. Do make sure that when you bend the patterns into position you are not forcing an unnatural twist into them.

Press the plywood down with a featherweight pressure and *perpendicular to the face of the plywood*—if you are edge-setting your pattern it will spring straight when it is removed from the boat and the resulting plank will not fit.

Now you are ready to spile the garboard; pause and sharpen your pencil. Choose a parallel-sided chip of wood perhaps one inch long, and wide enough to bridge the widest gap between your pattern edge and the rabbet. Unsheath thy sharp pencil (it is not quite Chaucer although we are entering the irresistible fray), hold thy chip of wood firmly against the keel side and scribe forth (and aft).

The midships section is straightforward because the plank is almost square to the keel. Aft, things get trickier because of the increasingly obtuse angle between the keel and the plank. Make sure that the chip is flat on the plank and that the lower corner of the chip is firmly pressed

12.1: Making the pattern

12.2: Making the pattern

12.3: Block of wood for spiling

12.4: Block of wood for spiling

against the keel. Forward, things get even trickier because the angle between keel and plank is increasingly obtuse and furthermore the rabbet is curved. This is the reason why the chip is only one inch long. The scribing of the rabbet around the forefoot will end up being a series of one-inch-long straight lines. That is fine.

Now that the lower edge has been scribed the upper edge must be marked; with your ruler on the upper mark at the midships mould, draw a neat and short line on the pattern, say two inches towards the keel from the upper mark. Label it '2in'. Later this line will tell you that the upper edge of the garboard plank is two inches from this pencil line. Repeat this at the stem, transom and the remaining moulds. Due to the curve of the rabbet, it is generally better to have a smaller measurement at the stem—say ½in. Gently remove the pattern and lay it on your planking stock without twisting or edge setting it. It is best

12.5: Block of wood for spiling

12.6: Pitching mark and steam bag clamp

12.7: Steaming the first garboard and spiling the second

12.8: Steaming the second garboard having fastened the first

12.9: Clamping during steaming

12.10: Dry fitting the forward end

to cut from quarter-sawn boards (boards with end grain perpendicular to the face) rather than the tiger grain boards from—presuming the tree has been sawn through and through—the top or bottom of the tree.

Tack the pattern onto the stock so that it cannot move. Firstly transfer the pitching mark. Sharpen your pencil. Using the chip of wood, transfer the marks from the pattern onto the planking stock. To do this line up the chip of wood with the marks on the pattern and, drawing on the opposite side of the chip, mark the planking stock. This line is where the chip was pressed against the keel.

From the 2in pencil line on the pattern, measure two inches and draw a line on the planking stock. Do this for the other mould upper edge marks and the stem and transom upper edge marks. Remove the pattern. Using a fair batten and some thin nails to guide it, join the upper

12.11: Steaming the after end

12.12: Boil in the bag with good inflation

edge marks and draw a pencil line. Allowing say four inches of additional length, cut the plank out with a circular saw. A circular saw tends to cut a fairer line than a jigsaw, which is liable to wobble. Be as precise as you can with the lower edge but do not remove the line.

You might want to allow ⅛in extra for the upper edge unless you are very confident. This is a contingency and may be used up on the lower edge in the final fitting. At the forefoot you will probably need to use a jigsaw because of the curve. Fair with a no. 4 plane or a block plane so that the lower line is just visible.

The hard work making the rabbet square now pays dividends, because the plank can be cut square and will fit into the rabbet; had the rabbet not been square a complicated winding bevel would have been needed on the garboard edge; such a tricky winding bevel would most likely come with a leak guarantee. Fair the top edge

12.13: Clamping in the aft end when steamed

12.14: Clamping in the aft end when steamed

of the plank so that the line is sweet. Mark the pitching mark onto the edge of the plank and put it through the thicknesser to the finished dimensions. Transfer the pitching mark back onto the face. Take a wire gauge (light swipe with the block plane to remove the sharp corner) off the lower inside edge of the plank. This will stop the sharp edge preventing the plank going home if the inside corner of the rabbet is not perfectly clean. Put a ⅛in chamfer on the top inside edge of the plank. This will prevent any sharp edges catching and tearing along the grain during the life of the dinghy. Line up the pitching mark on the plank with the pitching mark on the keel. Clamp the plank to the midships mould.

Put on the steam bag from forward to just aft of the midships mould. It is worth knocking the sharp tip off the forward garboard end as this can puncture the steam bag. After fifteen minutes of steaming it may be possible to gently clamp the

12.15: Dry fitting the starboard garboard

12.17: Dry fitted and ready for glue

12.16: Dry fitting the aft end

forward end of the garboard towards the rabbet. Don't apply vigorous clamping pressure, just enough so that some of the tension or resistance is steamed out of the wood. During steaming prepare several clamps and pieces of offcut timber as clamping pads.

This is the moment to mention Little Gripper—an associate and then friend of many dinghy plank-to-stem fittings. Quiet and nothing to look at, Little Gripper always does the job. The source of Little Gripper is long forgotten although I believe he may have once been a new six-inch Bessey F clamp.

After half an hour (the rule of thumb is one hour per inch of thickness for steaming—in this case 20 minutes plus), pull off the steam bag. Whilst stamina and calmness in adversity will be needed for the build as a whole, in terms of technical ability we are now at the apex of the challenge. The first clamp goes on the forward mould with

12.18: Glue in the rabbet

12.19: Glueing the plank on

12.20: Glueing the plank on

12.21: Pulling the plank to the rabbet

12 Garboards

12.22: A nest of clamps

a pad between the plank and clamp, the second clamp goes on the top edge of the garboard at the forward end. A pad may or may not be used; bear in mind that later you will cut the plank rebate. If you are on the starboard side (remember it is upside down) between the mould and the rabbet push the plank in with your knee or shoulder and then clamp the last bit in tightly to the rabbet. The plank would rather not twist and bend so give it as much support as possible. Two minutes have passed since pulling the steam bag off. Don't be alarmed if it doesn't fit exactly. The main thing is to get the shape into the timber. If it needs pulling into the rabbet, one of the stem-to-stem knee fastening holes is a useful place to put a clamp without a foot.

It is likely it will need tapping forward a little; it is useful to put on the clamp without a foot before tapping it forward because this clamp tends to stop the plank being tapped too far forward and 'riding up' the rabbet. If the plank is tapped too far forward it is a pain because everything has to be released to nudge it back again. Having tapped the plank forward, get some more clamps on to pull it to the rabbet, particularly between the forward mould and the stem.

Bear in mind a clamp without a pad underneath the foot is likely to leave a black mark on the timber. Place your pads carefully. I have cracked a perfectly good plank with a carelessly placed pad. This meant removing the plank and starting again… again.

Whilst the forward end of the plank is settling down and cooling, put the steamer on the after end and repeat the process. Two or three

12.23: Fitted and ready for fastening

long F clamps are useful for clamping at the transom; use a piece of sandpaper folded in half to stop the clamp foot slipping off the wet plank.

Once steamed, leave the plank for a couple of hours. Release it at the stem and make small adjustments so that it fits well. Clamp it back into position and tap forward as necessary. Having fitted the forward end, leave the forward end clamped in position and fit the after end.

Check or update your pitching mark. Remove the plank and put some slow-cure polyurethane foaming glue into the rabbet. Fit the garboard back onto the boat and clamp the life out of it. This may seem non-traditional at this point. It is also non-leaky-breaky. This is the only plank that is glued along its length.

Once the glue has cured fasten the plank. It is worth leaving the clamp on the stem and the clamp on the transom until you have at least one nail in the ends of the plank. I have in the past put a nail in the transom nearest to the skeg, released the clamp and watched with horror as the plank cracked; this has also happened at the stem. It is pretty galling to have attained the perfect fit and then have to break the whole plank off, clean back the rabbet and start again. As the rabbet is unlikely to be exactly the same on both sides and you require a fag paper fit the process will have to be repeated for the other side. You will be able to use the pattern again; by turning it over it should be found to fit relatively well.

Take heart from the news that once you have cut the rabbet and fitted the garboard the two hardest parts of dinghy building have been overcome; if you can build a dinghy you can build a boat of any size as the greater the scantlings the more forgiving the materials; I would like to build the clipper *Thermopylae*.

13 Plank spiling and cutting out

A spiling board is used in order to find the shape of the plank: cut two strips of 3.6mm 'pattern ply' at say four to six inches wide; tack them to the moulds, transom and rabbet with wire nails. It may be that the plywood needs to be broken and reconnected in order to accommodate the sweep of the planking. Attach the strips of plywood together with a hot glue gun. Do not twist or mis-shape the plywood; gently bend it into the gap.

Careful spiling is the way to get planks that fit; if the plywood is distorted or edge-set during the spiling process this mis-shaping will be transferred to the planking stock and the plank simply won't fit. If you are unsure of your method, consider spiling and then cutting a practice plank out of some plywood. Check that the practice plank fits.

Once you are very confident with your method, slightly lift the spiling board at the sternpost (perhaps 1/8in). This will help to toe the top edge of the plank in to the transom. At the stem you could slightly depress the spiling board and this will help the planking flare a little as it comes towards the bow.

Having fitted the spiling board to the boat, lean underneath and trace the top edge of the plank below onto it. This will give you the shape of the lower edge of the new plank. Mark the mould positions and label them.

In order to record the shape of the top edge of the new plank, once the spiling board has been removed, measure the plank widths at the moulds and mark these onto it.

13.1: Plank bevelled in preparation for patterning

13.2: Piecing together a spiling board

13.3: Piecing together a spiling board

13.4: Piecing together a spiling board

Scribe the shape of the stem onto the spiling board with a block. Mark the position of the transom onto the spiling board. Take the spiling board off the dinghy without distorting it and carefully place it on the selected planking stock.

Using a parallel block, which could even be your block plane, transfer the lower edge of the plank from the spiling board to the stock. Mark the mould positions onto the planking stock. Mark the plank widths at the moulds, stem and transom. Join the dots with a fair batten. If any of the dots do not match up with the batten take a view: ¼in is probably fine—let the batten go fair. Any larger than ¼in and there is a problem somewhere. If it was say ½in, you could consider halving this between two moulds to get ¼in on each mould. In any event, this discrepancy would need to be accommodated later on. The sheer line is set and has to be met.

13.5: Pattern clamped to a mould

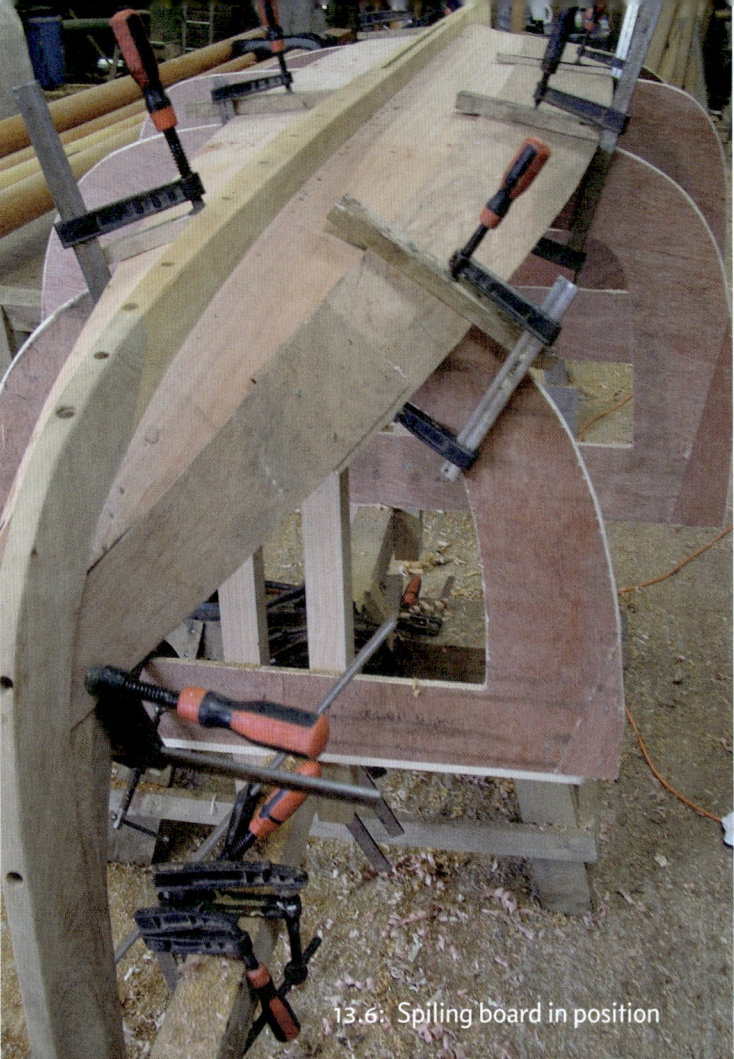

13.6: Spiling board in position

Remember that the widths need to remain correct at the stem. Cut the plank out with a circular saw (a circular saw keeps a fair line better than a band saw or jig saw). Fair and square the top and bottom edges.

Use this plank as a pattern for the plank on the other side. Make sure that both planks are the same size; it is easy for the second plank to be a little bigger than the first. Machine to the right thickness, which is normally ⅜in for a dinghy.

13.7: Spiling board in position

13.10: Scribing the shape by folllowing the top edge of the plank below

13.8: Spiling board in position

13.9: Spiling board in position

13.11: Using a parallel block plane to transfer the plank lower edge line

13 Plank spiling and cutting out

13.15: Connecting the upper mould marks or plank widths with a batten

13.12: Copying the line from the pattern onto the stock

13.13: Noting the plank widths at the moulds

13.14: Marking the stem angle onto the stock

13.16: Connecting the upper mould marks or plank widths with a batten

13.17: Draw round the spiled shape to get the plank for the opposite side

13 Plank spiling and cutting out

73

14 Planking

Clearly all elements of a well-built boat need to fit. This is of course crucial for the planking; if the planking does not fit the boat will leak. The following are general remarks about planking to supplement the spiling, cutting out, bevel and planking rebate details.

Plank steaming

The first four planks need steaming at the bow; above these there is little twist. Planks two and three often cup between the forward mould and the stem when steamed. If they do, on removing the steam bag clamp the plank between two pieces of batten at right angles to the grain of the planking.

Make sure the internal batten does not cross the landing onto the plank below. I have cracked the plank below in the past when trying to remove cup; a classic example of one small step forward and a giant leap backwards.

The first two planks need steaming at the transom because of the twist and hollow. In order to prevent these splitting along the grain a small piece of pattern ply underneath the clamp foot can spread the load.

Planks three and four do not tend to need steaming at the transom because it is relatively flat where the planks land on it; those above generally need steaming because of the twist and the curved shape of the transom.

Steam bag

To make a steam bag either source some wide plastic lay-flat tubing (ten inches wide and 125 microns should be fine) or take a sheet of thick plastic perhaps two feet wide, turn the edges over together and staple up.

Put the hose of a wallpaper stripper in one end and clamp the other end to the plank. A steam bag for dinghy planking need be no longer than five feet as only the ends of the planks are steamed.

The steaming process works best when the bag is inflated. It is often worth taking the sharp tip off the planking corners at bow and stern as these can tear the bag.

Plank fitting

The process is to steam and leave clamped in position for at least an hour; release the clamps and perfect the dry fit; glue and clamp up tight; allow the glue to cure properly and then fasten.

Ideally you will be so confident in your beveling and rebate work that you can gauge this by eye and it will not need adjusting. If that is the case, clamp the plank on midships at the pitching mark, fit and glue the stem, then work aft to the transom. If you have less confidence, it might be worth dry-fitting the whole plank from stem to transom prior to fastening the stem; this is because adjusting the aft landing from underneath whilst the plank is partially fastened to the boat may lead to a furrowed brow.

On rare occasions the fit at the stem is exact off the spiling board; on all other occasions the fit at the stem will need to be adjusted to the required 'fag paper' tolerance.

Clamp the plank onto the midships mould, lining up the pitching mark. Clamp the plank onto the forward mould and then bend into the stem. Make sure the lower edge of the plank fits tightly into the landing. Now the forward end of the plank can be scribed from the rabbet.

Let the forward mould clamp off and spring the plank clear of the rabbet; adjust the forward end of the plank with a sharp block plane; clamp back into position. Head to the back of the boat and give a light but firm tap on the end grain of the plank that is flying over the transom; this will drive the plank forward into the rabbet.

Plank gluing

Glue the plank into the rabbet at the stem and onto the transom. The simplest glue to use seems to be Gorilla glue. It is also worth running the glue up the landing for up to six inches. This ensures that the landing stays tight together. Make sure all parts with glue are clamped tightly together until the glue has set; once set the clamps can be released and the fastenings introduced.

Plank chamfers

Before fitting to the boat take a chamfer off the inside top edge and the outside bottom edge of each plank excepting the sheer and the garboard. Very sharp edges are liable to tear up and will not hold the oil, varnish, or paint very well.

Planking bollow at the transom

Those planks that fit to a convex curve in the transom will need a little bollow put in the plank otherwise it is likely to crack when clamped around the transom. This can either be done with a bollow plane, which is the best dedicated tool for the job, or failing that the forward roller of a belt sander, which will give a rougher finish.

Plank clamping

Leave a little of the plank below hanging over the transom. This is useful in order to clamp the next plank tight into the rebate and up against the previous plank. This clamping is further assisted if you cut the previous plank landing off flush with the transom. This also allows you to see the end grain of the landing and check that the fit of the two planks is tight.

Put a piece of timber batten underneath each clamp foot and at right angles to the planking grain on the outside of the boat. This spreads the load of the clamp foot and also prevents it leaving a black mark on the timber, particularly where the timber has been steamed. These battens might be say eight inches long and 1¼in square. A further piece of timber batten should be used under the head of the clamp inside the boat and at right angles to the planking grain.

This internal batten should reach onto the inside of the plank below, covering no more than an inch of it, which is equal to a little more than the plank landing. If the internal batten goes further down, the pressure when tightening up may crack the plank below. The battens mean that that the clamp jaws do not have to be full planking width.

A clamp without a foot can be useful in order to pull the plank up to the previous plank at the stem. The clamp screw is put in one of the stem to stem knee fastening holes. This vertical clamp is also useful when tapping the plank forward into the rabbet as it prevents the plank being driven too far forward and riding up the rabbet. Be careful not to damage the top edge of the plank.

If clamps are running short, scissor clamps can be made from pine with two 10G nails riveted through the top to stop them splitting. If the clamp is slipping when clamping the plank to the transom, a piece of sand paper folded in half can prevent this.

Planking shape and grain

The garboard is relatively straight. Planks 2, 3 and 4 curve down. This is most pronounced on 2, reducing in 3 and 4. It is easy to get a hook in the planking on 2, 3 and 4 which can make her look a little sad mouthed.

Follow the planking marks and keep looking at the bow of the boat to check the planking runs are fair between the forward mould and the stem. Planks 5 and 6 don't know where their loyalties lie and have an S-shape. Planks 7 and the sheer curve up or have a smile. It is best to have the grain following along the length of the plank.

Unless you have managed to source a tree that is bent with the exact curve that you need, having the grain flowing perfectly along the planking is rarely possible throughout a small dinghy. Keep an eye on the grain when you are laying out your spilling boars and take a middle road or route of best compromise, as a diplomat would positively advise.

Cove line

A router bit as pictured will make a very neat cove line if set up with a guide to run along parallel with the bottom of the sheer plank. The cove line wants to be ½in wide and the bottom edge 1½in above the bottom edge of the sheer.

Terminate the cove line nine inches from the stem and the same from the transom. There are two 'dots' at either end of the cove line. The centres of these are 1½ inches and 3 inches from the cove line end. The last dot is extended to a point 2 inches from the dot. The cove line is routered into the sheer plank before the sheer plank is fitted.

14.1: Steam bag aft

14.2: Steam bag at the transom

14.3: Glue in the land ending and rabbet

14.4: Bollow in plank end at the transom

14.5: Initial clamps on moulds

14.6: Pitching mark

14.7: Clamps and scissor clamps

14.8: Scissor clamps

14 Planking

14.9: Clamps and battens

14.10: Clamp sandpaper and batten

14.11: Clamping sand paper

14.12: Clamping the glue tight at the stem

14.13: Vertical clamp at the stem

14.14: Clamping the sheer at the transom

14.15: Using the plank below to clamp the rebate tight

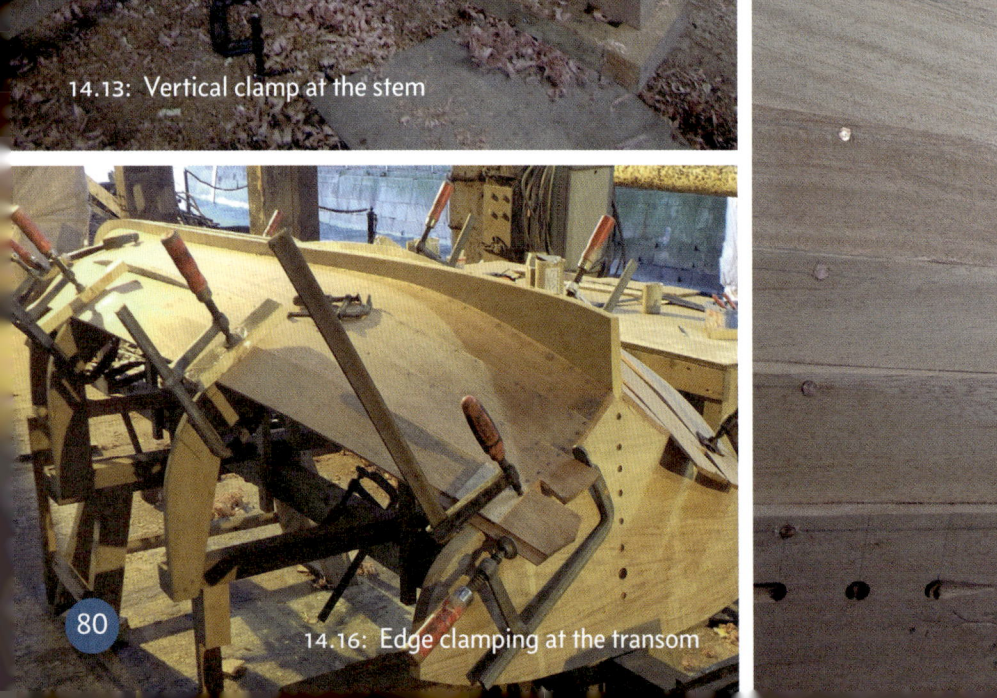

14.16: Edge clamping at the transom

14.17: Clamping and glueing the sheer plank

14.18: Planking at the turn of the bilge

14.19: Plank fastened forward and ready for steaming aft

14.20: Shape of a bilge plank

14 Planking

14.21: Planking at transom

14.22: Close up of planking grain

14.23: Cove line router cutter

14.24: Routing the cove line with a guide

14.25: Planking almost complete

14.26: Planked up and turned over

14 Planking

15 Plank lands

A rule of thumb for planking land width is twice the thickness of the planking; thus if the planking is ⅜in the lands will be ¾in. The plank land bevel is dictated by the moulds and faired in between the moulds.

Set the combination square or your thumb to ¾in and run a pencil line down the plank. This line marks the lower edge of the plank landing.

In way of the moulds, bevel off the outer corner of the plank until a straight edge touches from the pencil line marking the lower edge of the plank landing to the mark on the mould for the top of the next plank up. This is sometimes not possible due to the curve of the mould; in this case bevel according to the point where the straight edge touches the mould. The bevel will be different at each mould.

Look along what remains of the top edge between moulds and bevel off for a smooth run into the bevelled areas at the moulds. If the winding bevel isn't fair fore and aft, the planks won't fit together properly. And the landing that you are making must be flat athwartships. If it has a bump in it, the water will be kept out by ⅛in of bump rather than ¾in of well fitted, surface swelling landing.

A no. 4 plane works well for shifting material at the start of the bevelling. It seems to be best to finish with a block plane. If there is a minor wobble that you are having trouble eliminating, a wide chisel can be used as a scraper to iron out local bumps. If scraping, do be careful not to slip and dig an edge into either the landing or the visible part of the plank. It has been done and makes a scar that is difficult to erase.

The plank above remains full and square on its lower edge, so all of the change of angle of the hull has to be accommodated in the bevelling of the top edge of the plank below.

Whilst in the yard I expect the bevel to be perfect first go and any plank after the garboard to go up first time and never be removed; I am trying in a haphazard and rather ill-thought out way to put food on the table. However, if the challenge is not commercial, it is recommended that until total confidence is gained, bevel cautiously. It is better to take off too little than too much.

It is normally relatively straightforward to get the bevels correct for a distance forward and aft of the mid-ships mould. There is often some difficulty with the bevels between the forward mould and the stem and between the after mould and the transom. For a greater degree of certainty in these areas, bevel a little less than is needed and then dry fit the next plank.

At the dry fit stage the gap on the outside between the two planks will show how much timber still needs removing. If things go wrong

15.1: Marking out the land width

15.3: Checking the land bevel

15.2: Bevelling the lands

and too much is removed there are two ways out. You can ignore the ¾in land mark and spread the bevel further into the plank below; this reduces the acuteness of the bevel angle. Or if this is not possible, a bevel can be put on the inside of the plank above. This is a little complicated. A third possibility, when it is all too late and the plank is half attached, is to play the steamer over the internal plank land and gently clamp up. This will only alleviate minor gaps.

In all events, it is simplest and best to get the bevel right on the plank below. Once one starts messing around with adjustments things get complicated and a lot of time can be lost.

Planking rebates

Clinker planking must be smooth at both stem and sternpost. There is nothing worse than seeing bottom edges of planking proud at the stem, or a transom with a series of chines. There are

15.4: Land with a bump

15.5: Land without a bump

15.6: Marking a rebate

15.7: Marking a rebate

different ways to achieve this. The best method is perhaps more involved than the others but does create a better job in terms of strength and longevity.

The plank fastened to the boat must have a rolling rebate cut into its top edge for a distance of perhaps eight to ten inches. The planking bevel must run into nothing at its top edge when it meets the transom and rabbet in order to let the plank above fit to the transom or rabbet. At the same time, on the plank fastened to the boat, the edge of the landing nearest the keel begins to be rebated from full planking thickness where the rolling rebate starts until it is approximately half of the thickness of the planking at the transom or stem. This rebate is then deep enough for the plank above to accommodate a nail head punched in flush. This winding bevel must be fair and flat.

The final preparation is difficult to do with a

15.8: Planking rebate in lower plank at transom

15.9: Cutting the rebate edge on the bench

normal rebate plane or even a bull nose plane as the plane blade digs into the transom or the plane nose hits the stem. When a plane is no longer of use, take a sharp chisel the width of the land and use it as a plane; then when it is almost there make it flat and fair by scraping with the chisel.

The new plank that is to be fitted above must have a corresponding winding bevel on its underside for eight to ten inches (but no rebate) so that when the two are put together at the stem or transom their combined width is that of the planking.

Cut this winding bevel on the bench. Again, it must be flat and fair. Take nothing off at the bevel's start point and increase until it leaves approximately half of the plank thickness at the lower edge of the plank where it reaches the transom. This will correspond to the half plank thickness rebated into the plank below and the 'fag paper fit' will be successfully achieved.

15.10: Section through the rebates seen at the transom; these are not gaps, but close fits indicated with a marker pen; the unmarked rebates are difficult to see

Cut the forward plank rebates for the first two planks after the plank has been fitted and fastened. Although this is more difficult than cutting on the bench, as these planks are steamed and have significant twist, the plank would be liable to split on the landing if cut prior to steam bending. Cut the remaining plank rebates on the bench, which is easier. Use a tenon saw to cut the line of the rebate because it will give a straight edge. At the transom, if the upper plank is proud of the lower plank at the rebate, it can be faired off after glueing and prior to fastening. This would be unusual practice at the stem.

16 Bilge runners

The bilge runner protects the planking when the dinghy is ashore. It is fitted on a plank land so that it has a double thickness of planking underneath it, at a point where the timber is firmly against the planking on the inside.

This gives just over two inches of wood thickness, which sounds like a lot for a dinghy with ⅜in planking, yet is encouraging when one considers that the whole weight of the dinghy plus occupant will be shared between it and the keel when the dinghy is on the beach.

It is normally positioned at the bottom edge of the third plank, for perhaps 16 to 20 inches either side of the midships mould.

To check where the bilge runner is fitted on a dinghy of given shape, put a piece of straight wood with one edge on the keel and at right angles to the keel. Note where it touches the planking. This is the position for the bilge runner.

Choose a good piece of hard oak machined square, the same thickness as the land overlap. Each end should have a long taper to ³⁄₁₆in over twelve inches; chamfer the edges.

Fit the bilge runner during planking. Plan ahead when riveting on the plank underneath and leave one of the two nails in each timber bay undrilled. When the bilge runner is riveted on with one nail in each timber bay the effect will be uniform on the inside of the hull. Steam the bilge runner and cramp into position.

Drill a 3mm hole for the nails from the outside and at right angles to the hull. Rivet on with 13G by 1¾in nails. Later on the timber fastenings in this area will have to be longer as they will go right through the bilge runner.

Do not screw the bilge runner on. There is not enough wood thickness for a good fastening. In the years to come the screws will weaken their grip through knocks and bumps, and will themselves deteriorate and it will be difficult to do a really good job when trying to re-fasten them.

The copper nails riveted through will last as long as the other hull fastenings and if the bilge runner gets excessively chafed and needs replacement, grind or nip off the nail on the inside, knock off the rove, punch out and refasten in the same hole.

Another advantage of this method surfaces when you have to replace a cracked rib as the bilge runner doesn't have to be removed to get at the timber fastenings.

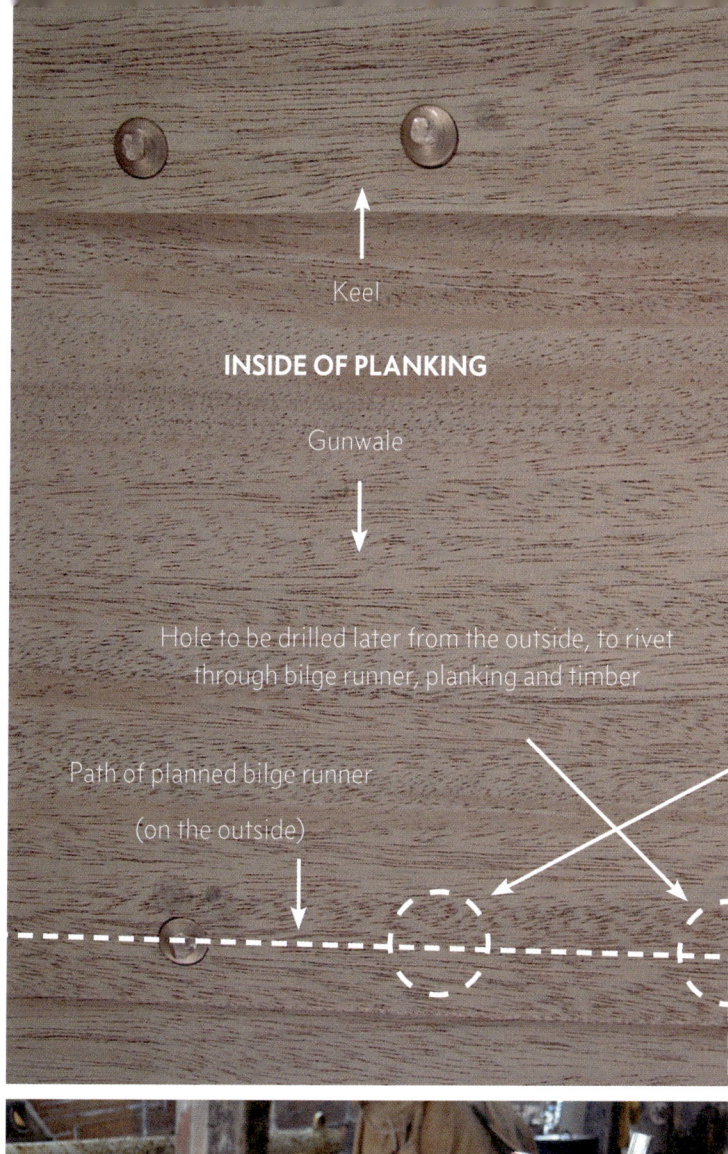
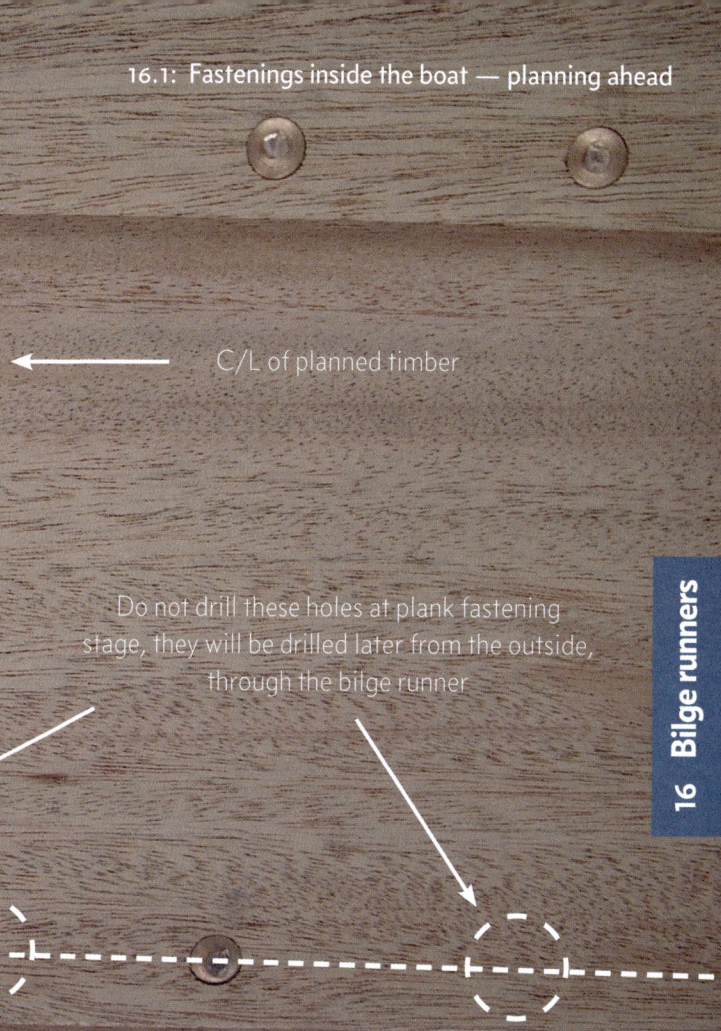

16.1: Fastenings inside the boat — planning ahead

Keel

INSIDE OF PLANKING

C/L of planned timber

Gunwale

Hole to be drilled later from the outside, to rivet through bilge runner, planking and timber

Do not drill these holes at plank fastening stage, they will be drilled later from the outside, through the bilge runner

Path of planned bilge runner (on the outside)

16 Bilge runners

16.2: Clamping the bilge runner into position after steaming

16.3: Clamping the bilge runner into position after steaming

17 Timbering

Select green oak which is free from knots and has a clear straight grain. We store all of our timbering oak in a pond. Tie a string onto it as green oak sinks. It is taken out the day before timbering and cut to the required dimensions.

Take a 'wire gauge', which is a very light chamfer, off the back edge. This reduces the probability of a grain peel-out on the outboard edge. Shape the inside edge as required. It is extra work but does look very good when the inside face of the frames is slightly rounded.

Clean the inside of the dinghy and sand off any marks; it is much easier to sand and clean before the timbers are fitted. Once, we varnished the inside of the dinghy prior to timbering; this was not a success as the hot timbers seared the varnish to the extent that the varnish blistered or lost adhesion in way of the timbers.

Take an old bandsaw blade of width suitable for timbers. Break it at the weld. Put it mid-ships in the dinghy and clamp it to the sheer plank. Check that it is midway between the keel to hog fastenings and the vertical columns of plank fastenings, and that it is upright at the sheer plank on both sides.

Once the blade is in position, make pencil marks against its smooth edge, on the keel and on each plank to show the route that one edge of the timber will take. Do this throughout the boat; it will be more awkward at the ends because of the twist, and less liable to be upright at the sheer.

Once the route of all of the timbers is marked, take a sharp pencil and a chock of wood half of the width of the timber, in order to mark where its centreline will be. Make this mark into some sort of a T so that you can distinguish this from the timber's edge.

Drill 3mm holes out from the inside through each landing where the timber marks are. Do make sure you are drilling on the centreline mark rather than the timber edge mark. Make sure that the hole is started in line with the existing nails and keep checking that the holes are coming out in line with the existing nails on the outside. Gently countersink all of the holes on the outside.

The timbering steam tube is made from lay-flat hose. Put it on a slight incline so that the timbers do not sit in a pool of condensed water. The hose can also be insulated with a blanket or old duvet. Put the hose of a wallpaper stripper in either end.

Steaming will work best if the lay-flat tube is inflated because then the steam will be under pressure and there will be no loss of heat through the tubing lying on the timber. Put perhaps six timbers in the steam tube at a time.

Clamp the gunwales temporarily outside the dinghy to back up the sheer, and clamp the mid-ships mould or a spreader bar inside. Gather a few clamps, a handful of 13G by 1in nails, a hammer, and a drill with a 3mm bit inside the boat. Gather another drill with a 3mm bit, lots of 13G by 1½in nails and a hammer outside.

This is a two-person job. Put on some welder's gloves and take the first timber out of the steamer. Be very wary of the steam, which can cause bad burns. Pass the timber to the person in the boat and close the steamer.

The 'insider' bends the timber down and puts a foot on it on the hog. They then deal with bending one end of it into the bilge while the person outside deals with the gunwale end.

Once the clamps are on the sheer (put some masking tape around the clamp foot otherwise the steel will blue the oak) the insider drills and taps in a central nail, making sure that the timber is on the marks previously made at the edge of the band saw blade.

Starting at the garboard, the 'outsider' drills up through the existing holes in the planking and through the timber. They then drive in a nail while the insider leans on the timber with a hammer-head wrapped in masking tape just above the nail hole. Both rush to the opposite side and repeat the process.

Any breakages can be used at the ends of the dinghy where the timbers butt up against the stern or stem knee. The clamps are not always used at the ends of the boat as the insider has to twist the timbers.

Mid-ships and aft it is a good idea to pop a timber offcut behind each timber's head before it cools as this helps to stop the timbers spreading the dinghy. Take them out when the timber has cooled. Forward, where the turn on the hog is sharpest, before bending the timber into the boat hold the bandsaw blade underneath its length. As the timber bends into the boat the blade becomes tighter and stops the timber breaking. Once in place winkle the band saw blade out.

Once the timbers are all in place and the dinghy looks like a fakir's bed, drill down through them as they cross the hog from inside. The hole should appear on the outside in line with the garboard fastenings on either side of the keel.

Before completing all of the rivets consider the risings, which are covered in a later chapter. Some of the timber nails also go through the risings.

Once the timbers have been riveted in, wedges will need to be put between them and the garboards to support that plank. Cut a handful from timber offcuts and fit one under each timber. Mark them all with a chock held next to the hog, and cut off at the mark so the drainage gap between hog and wedge is uniform. Put a dab of glue on the wedge and push it firmly into place. Then rivet through the timber, wedge and garboard.

17.1: Bow brace

17.2: Bow brace

17.3: Stern brace

17.4: Gunwales clamped outside and midships mould preserving the shape

17.5: Setting the route of the timbers with a band saw blade

17.6: Marking the route of the timbers on the side of the blade without teeth

17 Timbering

17.7: Marking the centre of the timber with a chock half the timber width

17.8: Planking fastenings with gap between for timber

17.9: Drilling the timber fastening holes

17.10: Timber fastening holes

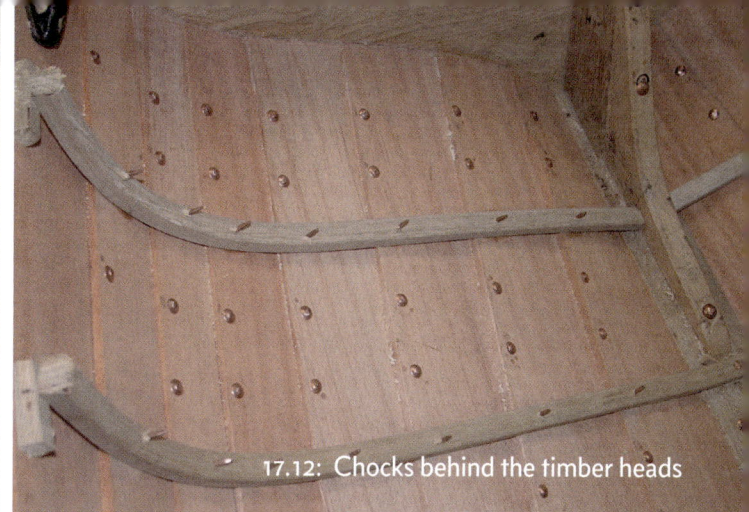

17.12: Chocks behind the timber heads

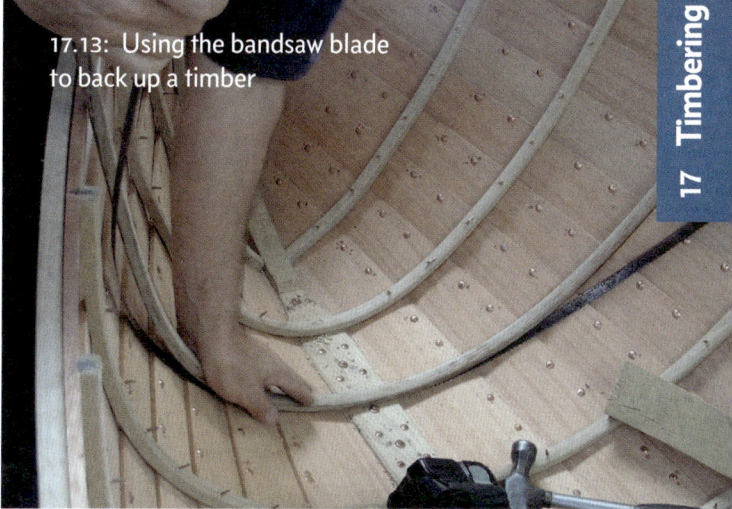

17.13: Using the bandsaw blade to back up a timber

17 Timbering

17.14: Backing up for the nails

17.11: Steam bag

97

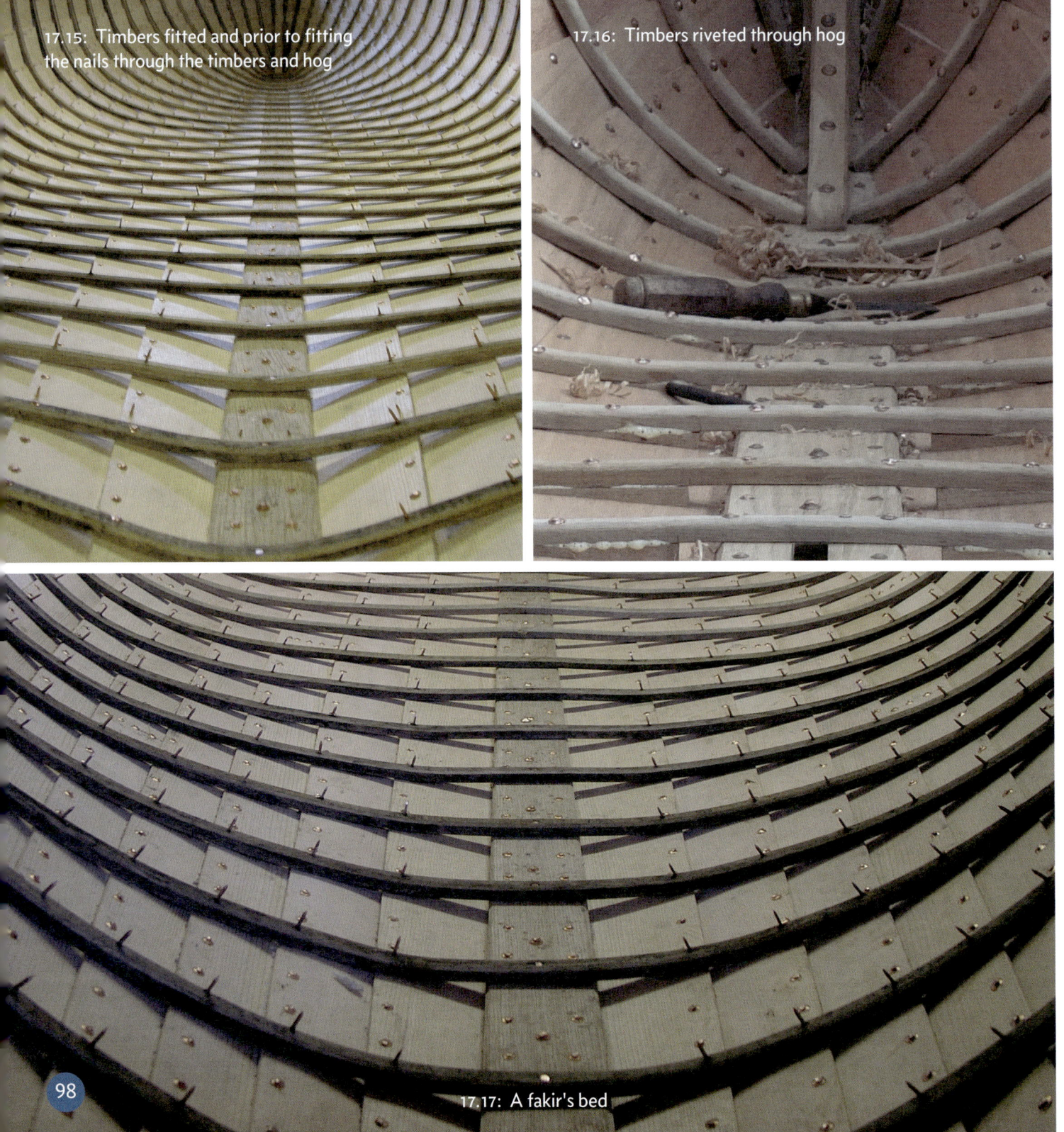

17.15: Timbers fitted and prior to fitting the nails through the timbers and hog

17.16: Timbers riveted through hog

17.17: A fakir's bed

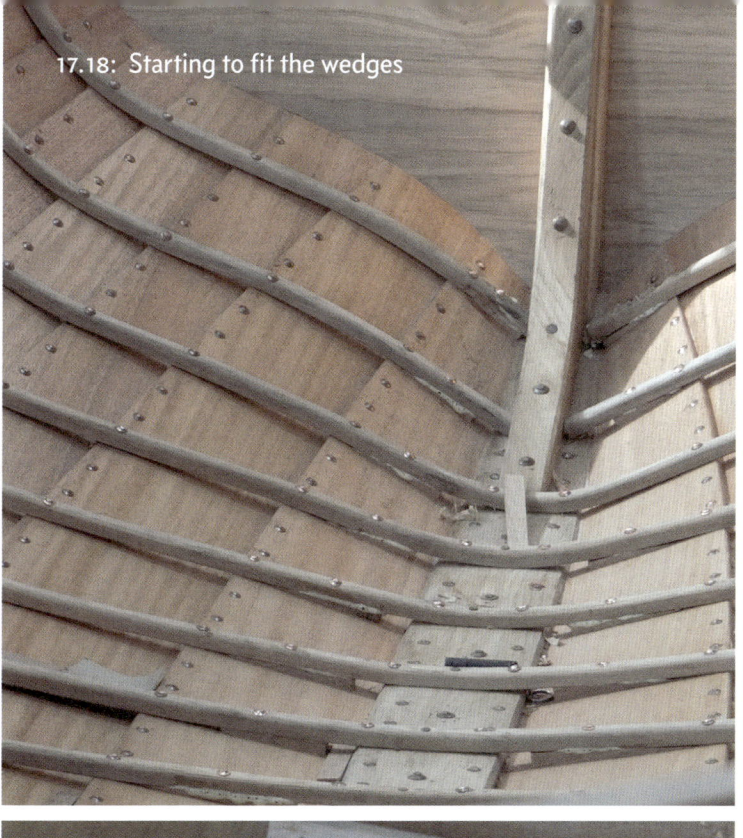
17.18: Starting to fit the wedges

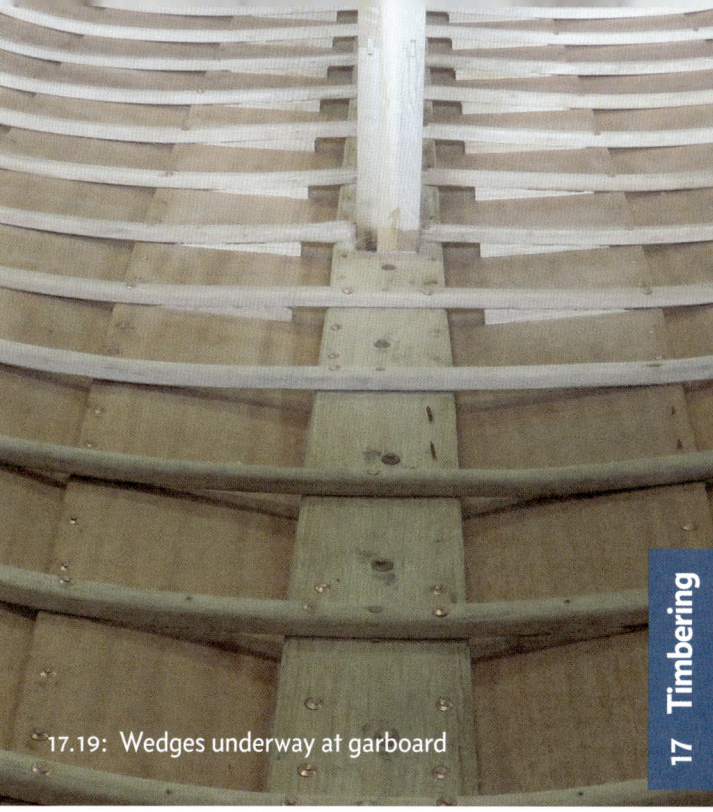
17.19: Wedges underway at garboard

17 Timbering

17.20: Wedges in a sailing dinghy where the timbers meet the centre case

17.21: A uniform limber gap between hog and wedges

18 Gunwale and rising

The gunwale* ('gunnel') is a band of wood fastened to the inside of the timber heads. In ships the gunwale was a thick plank underneath the gun deck. These thicker planks were also known as wales.

The name is a misnomer in a dinghy; unless your dinghy has significant tumble home in the topsides you are unlikely to be able to carry a cannon of sufficient size. 'Of sufficient size' is open to debate. Mounting an artillery piece of less than 12lb shot would be of little practical use when rowing off the Gulf of Aden.

Having machined each gunwale from a piece of timber longer than the dinghy, take its forward bevels against the stem, cut them and clamp the gunwale temporarily around the *outside* of the dinghy before timbering out. This backing up of the sheer will reduce the tendency of the dinghy to spread during timbering.

Once the timbers are steamed in, clamp the front end of the gunwale onto the inside of the timbers. To begin with, it can be handy to put the aft end in the sculling notch while doing this.

Put another clamp in the middle of the boat and let the end fly past the transom. Tap the gunwale forward so that it is touching the stem and clamp the remainder of the gunwale to the timber heads until it is not possible to clamp in any more owing to the end going over the transom.

With a straightedge in line with the transom top, mark across the top of the gunwale, and with the straightedge in line with the inboard face of the transom, mark the inboard face of the gunwale. Let the end of the gunwale spring out of the boat and cut it.

Bend into position inside the transom. It will be a little too long. Saw kerf it with the saw held flush against the transom. This may need to be done twice and will result in an excellent fit although there may be a few moments of irritation when the gunwale moves as it jams on the saw.

It is highly likely that two or three timber heads will be slightly out of line on each side of the boat. These must be straightened up for the visual effect of the boat and it can be easily done when fastening the gunwales.

In order to align the timber heads on the port side, stand on the starboard side. Start amidships and work aft or forward. Check that each timber head is straight and parallel. If one appears crooked, clamp the gunwale and plank together between two timbers and tighten gently until the timber in question is held tight. Tap the timber head forward or aft as necessary. Drill a 3mm hole and tap in the nail before releasing the clamp.

---

* This is called the inwale in some jurisdictions.

Incidentally, the gunwale is fastened with 13G by 2in nails with ⅜in roves. On a rowing dinghy the rivets go in the centre of the gunwale. On a sailing dinghy with a deeper gunwale the rivets are arranged up and down alternately.

The thwarts sit on top of the rising, the equivalent of a stringer on a larger boat. A rule of thumb in dinghies is to fit the top of the rising eight inches down from the sheer. Mark this point on each of the ribs; one method is to set a combination square at 8in and lay the handle part on top of the gunwale, marking a pencil line on the timber at the end of the ruler.

Risings are of different lengths depending on the thwart arrangement. If possible it is best to stop the rising before the last two feet of the boat because of the twist.

Measure the required length of the rising from the forward rib to the aft rib. Add four inches and cut the rising to length. Cut the rising to a 45 degree point at each end and bead both the upper and lower inboard edges. These details will be noticed by the discerning dinghy admirer.

The rising can be more awkward than the gunwale and should it need to go to the back of the boat it may need to be steamed because of the twist aft. If the rising is too long for the steam bag just steam the after end.

Whilst the wood is in the steamer prepare the boat for the rising, which needs to be fastened on at least every other rib.

Note the rib nails that will be behind the rising and knock them out. Clamp the rising into place. The clamp jaws will be too short. Use a ten-inch piece of offcut between the gunwale and the rising to extend the clamp jaws.

Inevitably there will be some places where the rising crosses a rib and needs a fastening, but there is fresh air between planking and rib. These areas are normally forward and aft and will need a small wedge, cut from a rib offcut, fitted between timber and plank. Without the wedge the plank is likely to crack as the rivets tightens up.

The rising is fastened, as for the gunwale, with 13G by 2in nails with ⅜in roves.

Some may recognize the saying, 'Measure twice cut once'. 'Think twice, drill once', is a similar but lesser known saying. Think before drilling a hole that comes out very close to the edge of a plank on the outside or close under a landing. Angle the drill up or down accordingly so that there is room for the nail head and riveting dolly.

18.1: Taking the bevel at the inboard face of the stem

18.2: Taking the bevel at the inboard face of the stem

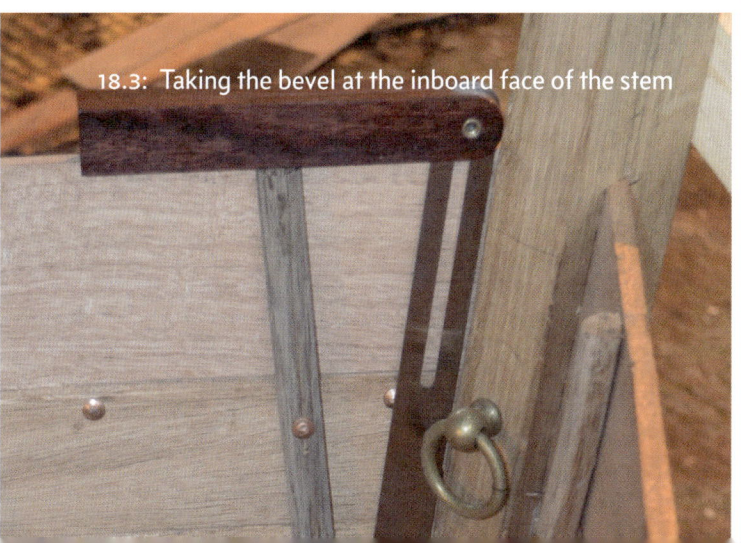

18.3: Taking the bevel at the inboard face of the stem

18.4: Port gunwale still in position for steaming timbers and starboard gunwale being fitted

18.5: Clamping the gunwales in and left long over the transom

18 Gunwale and rising

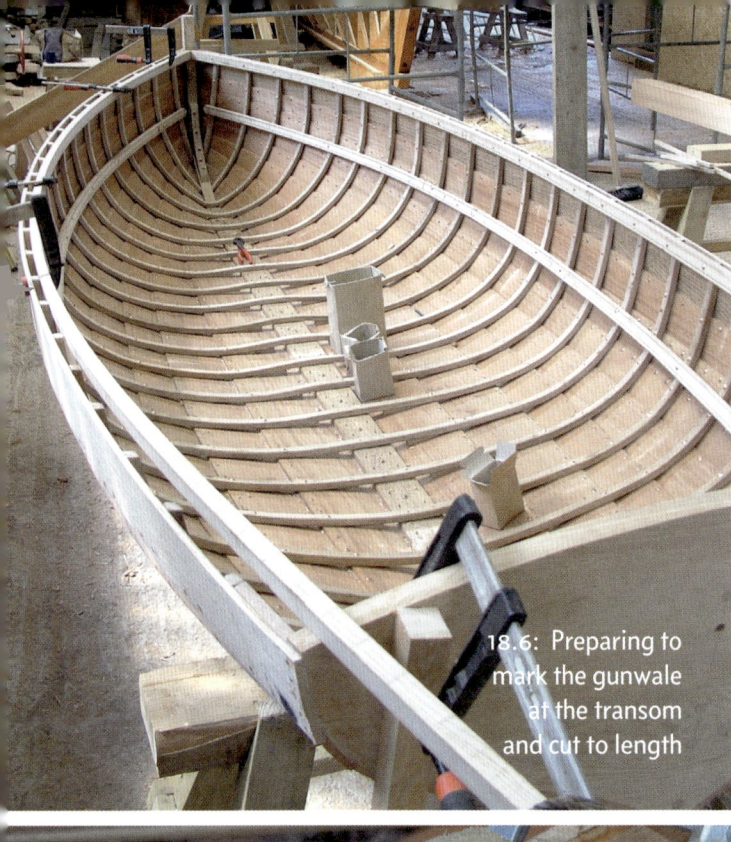
18.6: Preparing to mark the gunwale at the transom and cut to length

18.7: Gunwale cut a little long and sprung into boat

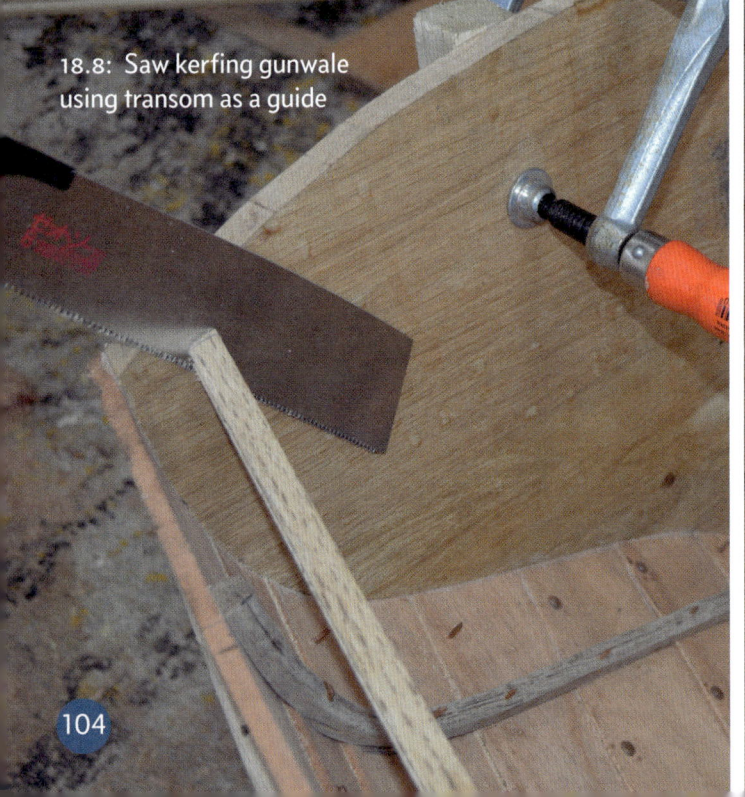
18.8: Saw kerfing gunwale using transom as a guide

18.9: Gunwale correct length

18.10: Wonky timber heads

18.11: Straight timber heads – clamped between timbers and tapped straight

18.12: Rising fastened every other timber

18.13: Rising end

18.14: Gunwales fitted

18 Gunwale and rising

19　Thwarts

The thwart should be fitted against two ribs so that it braces the dinghy apart. The timber centres are six inches and the thwart eight wide so the thwart will overhang the timbers. Make the overhang uniform.

Do not fit the thwarts around the ribs and up to the side of the boat. One day the boat will get rained on; the water will go into the gap between thwart and planking and be soaked up by the end grain of the thwart—with no ventilation the end grain will take a very long time to dry out. Damp will be held against the inside of the planking and it will go soft faster than it otherwise might have done. If the thwart is fitted to the inside of the ribs an air gap the thickness of the ribs is maintained between thwart and planking.

Choose two pieces of scrap timber a few inches shorter than the length of the thwart. Have two squares of thin plywood the width of the thwart, two small offcuts the thickness of the thwart and four clamps or a glue gun standing by.

This is a job for a person with three arms. Put one offcut the thickness of the thwart on the rising where the thwart will be. Hold the two long scraps of wood above the thwart thickness offcut and clamp or glue-gun the square of plywood underneath the two long scraps, having adjusted it so that the square of plywood touches both of the timbers against which the thwart will rest.

Do the same on the opposite side.

You now have the fore and aft bevel at each end of the thwart.

The plywood represents the top face of the thwart. With a sliding bevel take the vertical angle between the plywood and the rib.

Carefully take the pattern out of the dinghy and lay it on your piece of thwart wood (that has been pre-machined to thickness and width).

Mark the length of the thwart by scribing the outboard edge of the plywood at each end.

Set a jigsaw foot to the angle of the sliding bevel. Cut just outside the line and the thwart should fit perfectly first time with a little bit of pressure so that it is tight in the dinghy. If it is too tight, tickle it with a block plane.

The aft thwart against the transom is made up from billets fitted fore and aft. This saves timber by using short ends and also allows a longer thwart fore and aft which is more comfortable.

A thwartships bearer must be fitted a couple of timbers forward of the transom. This will be at the same height as the rising.

The bearer is half-lapped over the forward face of the timbers and then a screw put thought the bearer and into the timber.

A cleat is fitted to the transom either side of the stern post. The top of this is beveled so that it levels across from the bearer. There should be a gap of say ³⁄₁₆in beside the stern post to allow for drainage.

Spaces between the sections of thwart are approximately ¼in. They were once larger on a sailing dinghy and the mainsheet regularly jammed in a thwart gap, which was potentially dangerous.

The pieces are fitted from the centreline to outboard. Either a central piece is fitted with a cut-out and clearance of ¼in to go around the stern post, or two pieces are fitted with cut outs and a clearance of ¼in to go around the stern post and with the gap between the two pieces aligned with the centre of the stern post.

The forward ends of the billets that make up the thwart are wider than the aft ends. This causes the forward face to fan out and reduces the acute triangular shape of the outboard pieces.

The bevel on the underside of the outboard piece is always deep in order that the top edge of the thwart touches the timbers. Countersinking may also be needed to make divots in order to accommodate any rivets.

If the dinghy has side benches aft the outboard pieces become the side benches.

These side benches should be fitted before fastening the central thwarts in permanently. This will allow a little leeway in moving the central thwart ⅛in aft should the side benches come out slightly too short when jointing.

Either fit a cleat underneath the thwart to take the side bench or half-lap the side benches into the thwarts for a neat job.

If you are really visually aware the underside of the thwartships thwarts can be tapered. Mark a square the width of the thwart in the middle of the thwart. Taper ³⁄₁₆in from the edges of the square to the outboard end of the thwart. It is a bit of extra work but it does look good.

Fasten the thwarts to the rising with two 10G by 1¼in screws per side. On the central thwarts with two knees these fastening holes will be covered by the knees.

The thwart post, Atlas of the dinghy, is a small piece of wood with an important role. Cut a piece of timber rectangular in section (it will be longer fore and aft than it is athwart ships).

The thwart itself may not be parallel to the keel fore and aft. The marking up of the post must be done on the side of the thwart that is highest above the keel. Cut the bottom of the post square and hold it in the dinghy at right angles to the keel, with the top of the post against the edge of the thwart. Hold a straightedge fore and aft on the underside of the thwart and against the side of the thwart post. Mark the post along the top edge of the straightedge in order to get the bevel. Square across and cut.

Make the post elegant by cutting stop chamfers on all four corners, making sure that the chamfer ends well above the sole boards and well below the thwart.

As the thwart is centred on two timbers the bottom of the thwart post will land on a keel-to-hog fastening between the two timbers. (The keel fastening will locate the post without the need to cut a mortice in the hog, which may weaken the hog and will certainly provide a good spot for water to sit and make the wood soft). Countersink the bottom of the post; the central sole board which is fastened down will stop the post turning.

19.1: Long offcuts resting on thwart thickness offcut

19.2: Clamp the plywood below the long offcuts

19.3: Taking the bevel of the timber from the plywood

19.4: Pattern laid out on thwart wood

19.5: Setting the jig saw to the sliding bevel

19.7: Bearer for aft thwart

19.6: Fitted thwart

Set a screw in at an angle through the heel of the post and making sure it avoids the rivet in the keel. Make sure that the post doesn't 'creep' out of line as you tighten the screw. Having marked the post on the side of the thwart highest above the keel, it will be slightly too big. Tap it in, giving a little crown to the thwart. Put a gripfast nail or screw through the thwart and into the post. The thwart is now pushing down on the keel and will prevent the keel from hogging in the future. By slightly opposing the keel and the thwart, the post has unified the structure, giving a tangible strength increase to the dinghy with a minute weight increase.

19.9: Gaps between tapered billets of aft bench

19.8: Fastenings in aft thwart bearer and transom thwart cleats

19.10: Fairing below aft thwart

19.11: Half laps of the side benches into the thwarts

19.12: Sailing dinghy side benches with cleat underneath

19.13: Tapered thwarts

19.14: Fitting Thwart Post

19.15: Thwart post giving camber to thwart

19 Thwarts

20 Knees

Knees are an immediate indication of the boatbuilder's ability to make good looking shapes.

Ideally one would like to use an oak crook. However, in these honest times, crooks are pretty hard to come by and also must be well seasoned before use, particularly if there is to be some confidence that they will not be caught. Half-lapping is a reasonable alternative and has the added benefit of being economical in timber use. Thwart knees should be one inch thick. Machine timber appropriately, half-lap and glue together.

Consider the orientation of the knees so that the joints will all appear uniform port and starboard. For example you may want to see the horizontal joint of the half-lap when looking at the dinghy from forward and the vertical joint when looking from aft. In order for this to come about the port side half-laps will have to be cut in the opposite orientation to the starboard side.

Each central thwart has two knees per side, the forward thwart one knee and the after thwart no knees.

At each bay between the ribs where a knee will be located, fit packer up between the gunwale and planking. If this is forgotten, when the rivet is tightened in the knee head it may crack the plank, as the plank can be pulled into the fresh air between the plank and gunwale.

Plane the underside of the knee foot flat. It may also have to have a slight bevel. Push it outboard until it touches the gunwale and clamp it in position.

Make a chock of wood the size of the gap between the inboard face of the gunwale and the inboard face of the planking. Use this chock to trace the shape of the boat onto the knee. This can also be done with a pair of dividers.

Cut out to the line. The knee on the forward thwart will be square to the hull and is easy to cut on the bandsaw. The knees on the central thwarts will have a bevel where they touch the hull because they lined up with the thwart which is square to the centreline yet the outline of the boat is a curve.

Either use hand tools, a jig saw with a bevelling foot, or bevel the bandsaw bed. Inevitably, getting the knee bevels to fit is time consuming.

Fit all of the thwart knees before shaping the curved face. Shape one knee and use it as a template for the others.

The head of the knee is square; it stands proud inboard of the gunwale $\frac{7}{8}$in. The body of the knee must not be parallel with the planking otherwise it will seem too upright. It must gradually increase in width until it curves into the foot which is gradually tapering, narrow and long; in essence it must be elegant.

A sanding drum in a drill is useful to smooth the curve of the knee; knobbly knees are never attractive. Put a light chamfer on the edges of the knee.

Once the knees are shaped a pair of 13G rivets must be put through the half-lap so that should the glue fail in several decades time, the knees will hold together and do their job. Consider the orientation of the rivets so that they are all facing the same way.

Glue the knees into the boat. This will serve two purposes: firstly it will prevent water wicking under the knee and sitting atop the thwart which will eventually lead to decay, and secondly it will make it much easier to fasten the knee in the exact position that you want it to sit.

Check the double knees from the opposite side of the boat to ensure that they are parallel and also to ensure that the gap between the knee and the edge of the thwart is parallel.

To fasten the foot of the knee, drill down through knee and thwart. Make sure that the fastenings in the knees are all drilled the same distance from the knee's toe.

Lightly countersink and drive a 10G 2½in or 3in nail down through knee and thwart. Leaning on the nail head, clench or bend the nail over into the grain underneath the thwart. This is a neater method than riveting; nobody likes to see a pair of limpets on a thwart foot.

To fasten the head, drill outward angling the drill down slightly so that the nail head is below the upper rubbing strake. If the knee is one of a pair drill its neighbour at the same time, making sure that the angle of the drill is the same so that the nail heads are in line on the outside. Rivet the knee head with a 10G nail and $7/16$in rove.

In the plank below the sheer plank, drill through from the outside of the boat into the back of the knee. Countersink the hole and drive in an 8G by 2in bronze gripfast nail. If the dinghy is a larger sailing dinghy she may also need a second gripfast nail through the sheer just above the cove line.

As with the thwart knees, the gunwale must be packed out in way of any breast hook or quarter knee fastenings. The quarter knees have two rivets in each arm. The arm along the transom is slightly longer than that on the gunwale. The arm on the transom must be lifted slightly above level. If level, the quarter knees look like the ears of a sad dog—downcast.

The breasthook has two rivets in each arm. To look right the breasthook arms must be longer than one might think they need to be: twelve inches for a breasthook arm is not too long. If she is a sailing dinghy she must have an additional rivet through the stem head and centre of the breasthook. The arms of the breast hook and quarter knees need to be long and tapering.

20.1: Timber marked for a half lap

20.2: Half lap cut

20.3: A clutch of knees ready to glue together

20.4: A knee glued and clamped

20.5: A clutch of knees glued together

20.6: A knee glued together

20.7: Fitting a knee

20.8: Shaped and riveted

20.9: Shaped and riveted

20.10: Quarter knee with rivets

20 **Knees**

20.11: Forward thwart knee

20.12: Glueing the knees into position

20.13: Nail ready to clench under thwart

20.14: Single rivet through knee head

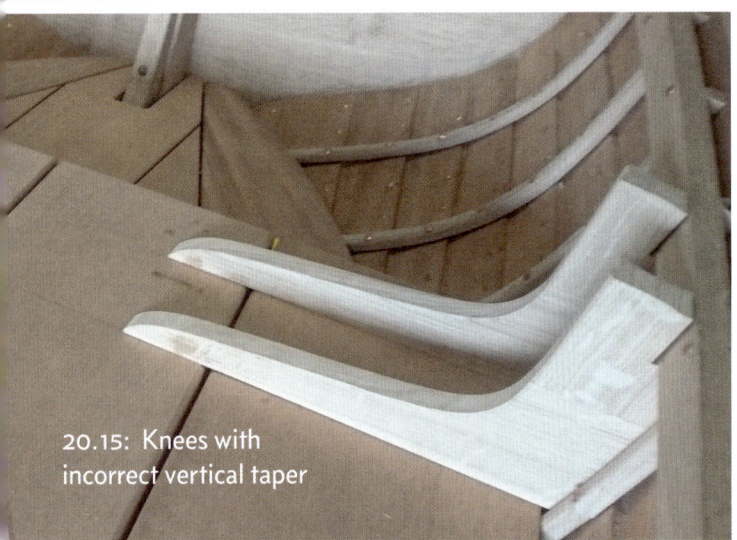
20.15: Knees with incorrect vertical taper

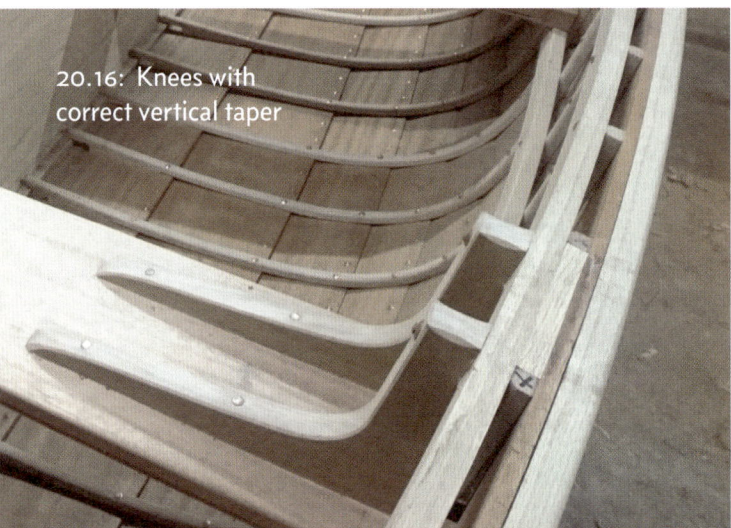
20.16: Knees with correct vertical taper

20.17: Grip fast nails in sheer and plank below on large dinghy

20.18: Grown Oak knees

20.19: Half lapped knees

20.20: Sailing dinghy quarter knee

20 Knees

21 Rubbing strake and capping rail

With much of the work on a boat, planning and preparation begins long before shaping and making.

Prepare four full-length rubbing strakes, approximately the width of the plank landings, or for lightness of eye ⅝in by ¾in.

Round off the outside edges so that when fitted the rubber will be ⅝in high with ¾in sticking out from the side of the boat.

Lower rubbing strake

When fairing in the planking at the transom to eliminate multiple chines, leave the bottom edge of the sheer plank full. The curvaceous transom shape visually ends at the lower rubbing strake and this will be fitted with greater ease and neatness if it doesn't have to twist round in the last three inches.

Initially only fasten the sheer strake on with one fastening per rib bay. The second fastening will go through the lower rubbing strake after the ribs have been fitted.

Measure the angle that the lower rubbing strake will make with the stem using a bevel. Clamp it in place and tap it forward until it meets the stem. A saw kerf at the stem may be necessary to get a perfect fit. If you are single-handed, it helps to put a cramp from top to bottom of the sheer plank at the transom so that the rubbing strake can go through the cramp and be loosely supported.

Fasten the strake at the stem first, with a 12G by 1in gripfast nail. Follow the line of the sheer plank so that both bottom edges are flush. This will help ensure that the rubbing strake is fair.

Use a long 3mm drill bit to help sighting up, look over the gunwale to line up with the landing fastenings below and drill through the centre of the rubbing strake from the outside. Try and make sure that the new hole is the same distance below the inside top edge of plank seven as the existing fastening.

Tap a 13G by 1¾in nail through and rivet up with a ⅜in rove.

Upper rubbing strake

Measure the angle that the upper rubbing strake will make with the stem using the bevel. Clamp the strake in place and tap it forward until it meets the stem. A saw kerf at the stem may be necessary to get a perfect fit. As with the lower rubbing strake, if you are single-handed it helps to put a cramp over the sheer plank at the transom so that the strake can go through the cramp and be loosely supported.

Fasten the rubbing strake at the stem first, with a 12G by 1in gripfast nail. Follow the top line of the sheer plank so that the top edge of the strake is flush with the sheer. This will help ensure that the rubbing strake is fair.

The upper rubbing strake is fastened with gripfast nails into every other timber head. Once it is clamped into position work from forward to aft and drill adequate clearance and pilot holes at every other frame. Drill from slightly forward and at an angle so that the gunwale fastening remains intact. The pilot holes must be correct in order to avoid splitting the sheer plank or timber head. Fasten with a 12G by 1¼in gripfast nail.

Capping rail

The capping rail is a relatively quick job. Take an offcut of planking up to six feet long. Fit one end aft around the transom and mark underneath using the inboard face of the gunwale as a guide. The upper edge of the capping should come more or less flush with the transom top and the transom can be faired down to the capping.

Cut to the line then set the combination square to 2in and follow the curve to give an outside edge. Cut to the new line, fair in and cut off square at the forward end.

Cut a two-inch long nibbed scarph at the forward end. With a spokeshave make a light chamfer on the inboard lower edge. Fit with this edge overhanging the gunwale by ⅛in.

Drill with a 10mm spade bit every four inches, staggering the holes from side to side with two fastenings in the scarph ends (one inboard and one outboard).

In timber this thin the spade bit will cut both clearance and pilot hole. Fasten with 6G by ¾in bronze countersunk wood screws and plug the holes. Repeat the process for central and forward sections. Fair in the scarph sides and lightly round the capping edges.

Before fastening cut an exact copy for the other side. It may be that the two sides are not exactly the same. With a little delicate sideways clamping a capping patterned on one side can be edge set and made to fit both sides.

When fitting the final section, fit the joint around the stem first and let the aft end fly over the scarph cut in the forward end of the central section.

Once the forward end is fitted around the stem and clamped in position the after end can be marked. Cut the after end with at least ¹⁄₁₆in spare beyond the mark. A little more can always be taken off but if it is too short it will either be a long term embarrassment or you will have to make another piece.

21.1: Lower rubbing band bevel

21.2: Fitting the lower rubbing band

21.3: Fitting the upper rubbing band

21.4: Upper rubbing band fitted

21.5: Rubbing bands at stem

21.6: Rubbing bands at transom

21 Rubbing strake and capping rail

21.7: Making the capping from planking offcuts

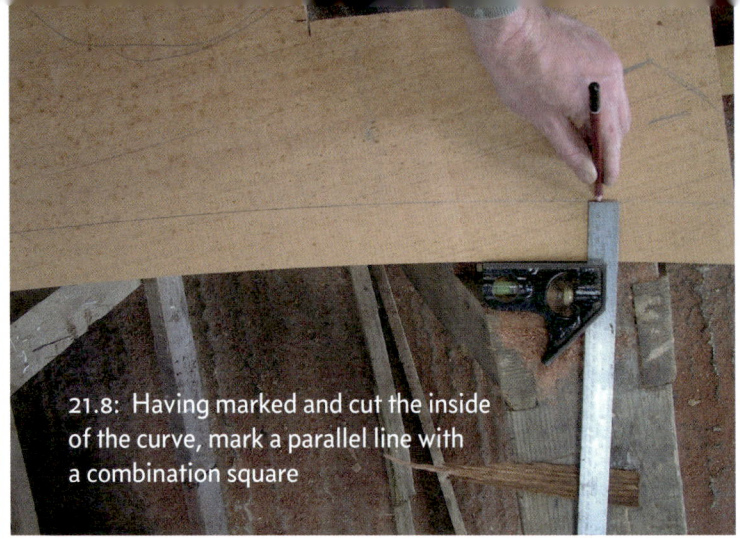

21.8: Having marked and cut the inside of the curve, mark a parallel line with a combination square

21.9: Nibbed scarph in the capping rail

21.10: Capping at transom

21.11: Capping complete

22 Rowlocks

The rowlock will be eleven inches aft of the aft face of the thwart. Dinghy size rowlocks have a ½in stem and are made in bronze or galvanized steel.

Glue a timber offcut up between the gunwale and planking so that it sits between the timber heads in way of the rowlock, whose plate sits on top of the capping. It is better not to let the rowlock plate in flush because this will expose end grain and the water will inevitably get under the varnish in the future causing darkening of the wood.

Bore a hole in the middle of the capping with a 20mm Forstner bit, deep enough but no deeper than the depth required to take the spigot of the rowlock plate.

Rivet a piece of wood ¾in thick, five inches long and 1½in wide, with some curve on the inboard face, onto the inside of the planking ¾in below the gunwale (a piece of frame offcut can be used as a temporary spacer) and centred fore and aft on the 20mm hole in the capping. This lower piece of timber will hold the stem of the rowlock. It will have to be cut around a timber. Allow a ⅛in gap all around the timber and chamfer all edges.

Glue the rowlock stem holder into position with the spacer temporarily in place. Once the glue has set rivet through both ends of the rowlock stem holder with 10G nails. Although 12G nails might appear the right size, they were found to inconveniently sheer off under the pressure of rowing from Clovelly to Lundy.

Leave the clamp on whilst drilling and riveting to prevent breaking the glue seal. Put the rowlock plate in the hole in the capping and fasten temporarily with two screws. Using a 13mm drill bit bore through the rowlock plate and down through the stem holder. This will ream out the rowlock plate by 0.3mm so that the rowlock is an easy fit and turns freely.

22.1: Rowlock attachment components

22.2: Drilling through the rowlock plate

22.3: Rowlock arrangement before final fitting of the plate

22.4: Rowlock completed

23 Sole boards

Sole boards are fitted so that there is no point loading on the planking; the sole boards spread the weight over the timbers, which themselves distribute the weight over the planking.

There is a central fixed board and then a removable sole board port and starboard. The removable sole board is generally make up of three planks. The sole boards are full-length in a dinghy up to say twelve feet after which they are in two halves with the joint under a thwart.

Start by fitting the central board. It needs to be 1½in wider than the hog and is fitted in two sections with a butt joint around the thwart post. It is screwed in with 8G by ¾in slotted screws that sit in solid knurled brass screw cups set flush into the sole board.

The sole board cleats will locate under these central boards. Cut patterns for them out of some chunky timber that fit the inside of the hull every two feet and come out from the centreline as far as the sole boards will. Steam short lengths of ⅜ by 1½in planking offcuts and clamp them around these formers. This bends the shape of the hull into the sole board cleats. It is a good idea to exaggerate the curve of the formers as the steamed timber will spring back a little.

Cut a pattern for the inner or first plank of the sole boards out of some thin plywood and lay it in the boat alongside the central board. Bear in mind that the first plank needs to be approximately ⅜in wider than the second and third planks. The reason is explained below.

Cut the inner sole board plank out twice, one for each side. Fair and then chamfer the outboard edge. Don't worry about the ends for now.

Put the steamed bearers into the boat so that they tuck under the central boards for at least an inch. They will locate the sole boards and stop them moving fore and aft, but always leave a gap of ¼in between a rib and the bearers otherwise the sole boards may be awkward to remove.

Lay the first sole board into the boat. Check that the board is more or less close up with the central board. Drill a 2.5mm hole through the sole board and into each bearer. Do not drill all of the way through as you might go right through the boat.

Take the bearers and sole board out of the boat. Drill the holes right through the bearer and lightly counter sink the sole board. Tap 13G by 1in nails into the sole board so that they protrude a little, line up the bearer underneath and drive the nails right through.

Turn the board over and put the nail heads on top of a lump hammer head. Clench over the nails into the grain of the bearer. This first plank is always a fiddle because everything is swimming

23.1: Steam bending the cleats around the formers

23.2: Central board in a sailing dinghy

23.3: Propping the first sole board into position

23.4: Propping the third sole board into position

about. Put this board with attached bearers back in the boat. Prop it down underneath a thwart.

Using the outboard edge of the first pattern as a guide for the inboard edge of the second pattern, make a pattern for the second plank. This may need fettling once it is bent into the shape of the boat. Once it is fettled cut out two 'second planks', fair and chamfer both inboard and outboard edges. Put the second sole board in place. Check for a uniform gap or say ⅜in; perhaps put in three temporary spacers; prop down. Drill through the sole board and into the bearers. Take the lot out and fasten as before. Put the lot back in the boat and follow the same procedure for the third sole board plank.

Having attached the third plank put the board in place and mark the ends. This seems to be attractive if it rakes slightly from the central board so that the sole board end is not abrupt. To get from the end of the sole board to the side on

23.5: Sole boards dry fitted

23.6: Forward end of the sole boards

23 Sole boards

23.7: Batten and automatic button

23.8: Detail of baton and automatic button

23.9: Making the bow sheets

23.10: Underside of the bow sheets

23.11: Bow sheets

23.12: Bow sheets fitted

23.13: Making the stern sheets

23.15: Stern sheets

23.14: Stern sheets

23 Sole boards

23.16: Sole boards, bow and stern sheets

129

the corner of the third plank a teacup seems to be a good radius.

Cut off any excess cleat that comes out past the third sole board. Allow the cleats that protrude and go under the central board to be perhaps an inch long. A light chamfer on the top edge can assist the cleat sliding under the central board, as can a rub with a candle.

To make a neat gap between the removable board and the central one, mark a line from the inboard edge of the first plank that is the same as the fore and aft gap between the other sole boards. Using a 15mm Forstner bit drill a scallop on each side of the cleats except the forward side of the forward cleat and the aft side of the aft cleat. Cut away the timber between the scallops taking care not to cut off the cleats. Chamfer the fresh edge, and the sole board now has an even gap with attractive stops in way of the cleats.

It only remains to fit a batten in order to allow the 'automatic buttons' to have a place to be fastened. The batten could be ¾ by ⅜in and two timbers shorter than the sole boards (one timber bay at either end). It can be attractive to put a small ogee on the outboard side of the batten which gives some sentiment of the sole board edge flowing back into the dinghy. This batten is fastened in at each timber and the fastening plugged, with the exception of two fastenings which are left out in order that the automatic button can be fastened down through the batten and into a timber.

The gap between the batten and the sole boards should be approximately ¼in otherwise things get too tight and it is difficult to remove the sole boards.

If making a set of sole boards that will be chopped in half when complete make them full-length first, as although it is awkward removing them it makes it much easier to get fair lines between the boards. Make sure that you have a pair of cleats at the joint otherwise the plank ends of one sole board will be flapping about.

Bow sheets can be fitted forward of the forward thwart. These rest on the risings and are made from planking offcuts in a similar way to the sole boards, with a cleat connecting the boards and the nails clenched beneath the cleat.

Stern sheets can be fitted in the after well of a longer dinghy. Bearers one inch thick and 1¼ inches deep are fitted to the hull so they rest on the frames. These bearers are checked around the frames with at least one on the forward side of a rib and one on the after side so that the stern sheets are located. The bearers do not touch the hull.

Straight planking is nailed to the bearers starting outboard and working inwards in a reducing V-shape. A facing of similar shape to the facing underneath a smaller aft dinghy thwart can be fitted to the front of the stern sheets. If this is the plan allow the stern sheets planking to overlap the forward bearer enough to also overhang the facing piece. Shadow lines are attractive.

24 Odds and ends

The crown of the transom can be vulnerable. An early dinghy suffered a broken crown during use (having been run down by a 20-ton yacht). Given the circumstance this constituted minor damage. In order to improve the chance of leaving the scene of a collision at sea unscathed, an option would be to drive three long nails down into the transom on either side of the sculling notch.

Sculling notch

The sculling notch can be cut with a hole saw. For dinghies a hole saw with a diameter of 3in will suffice. Clamp a piece of scrap timber on the inside of the transom so that the hole saw does not break out the edges of the sculling notch. Measure two thirds the diameter of the hole saw down from the crown of the transom and centre the hole saw on the centreline of the transom. In this way the hole saw will naturally cut some return on the hole so that the sculling sweep is less inclined to desert its post.

The hole is drilled at right angles to the transom, the sharp edges of the return softened and then the whole chamfered.

The notch can be leathered if required.

Drain plug

The drain plug is generally sited in the garboard and in the timber bay immediately abaft the sole boards. The hole is drilled from inside using a Forstner bit with a brave soul holding a timber backing pad on the external plank in order that there is no break out. If there is any doubt over

24.1: Bronze gripfast nails in the transom crown

24.2: Drilling the sculling notch

24.3: Sculling notch with a return

24.4: Leathered notch for use when rudder unshipped

24.5: Drain plug

where the hole will appear drill through the planking with a very small drill bit to guide the way.

Once the drain plug has been dry fitted into the hole the three fastenings can be drilled. Have a mind for the grain of the plank and make sure that the holes do not line up along the grain as this can promote cracking.

Drive a nail in from the outside and rivet it into the countersink in the bronze fitting; this tends to be a 10G nail and the job is awkward.

Screwing the fitting into $\frac{3}{8}$in planking is not the done thing.

Fairleads

A wooden fairlead is a sculpture, tapered, moulded and shaped in every direction. It is as traditional as can be; strong, simple and aesthetically additive to the boat. This small piece of wood sums up the challenge of wooden boatbuilding: functional aesthetics. But for some it may be too traditional, in which case a bronze version serves equally well; in fact for my part I prefer the lipped and handed four-inch bronze fairleads.

The aft end of the wooden fairlead must be checked into the capping so that if aft or lateral load comes on the warp, it is not simply hanging on by its fastenings but is pushing against the capping, itself fastened to the gunwale and butted against the transom, fastened to … and so on.

Stemhead

The shape of the stemhead can be made to taste. We have passed through various incarnations and settled at a middle road. Initially the stem heads were cut flat with a little rake aft; this seemed rather abrupt. As a reaction they became exaggerated in the spirit of the Vikings. The current equilibrium is somewhere in between abrupt and Viking. It may be deemed moot that this is a fine line to tread.

24.6: Bronze lipped and handed fairlead

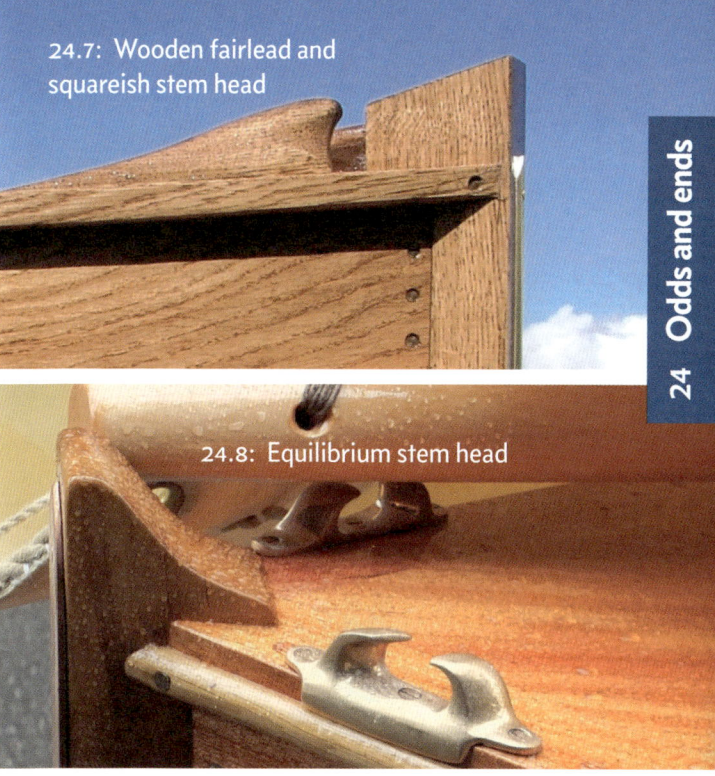

24.7: Wooden fairlead and squareish stem head

24.8: Equilibrium stem head

24.10: Checking the aft end of the fairlead into the capping rail

24.9: Viking stem head

25 Name carving

Find a set of letters in a typeface that you like. Letters of 1¼in height look right on a dinghy transom. Adjust the size using the percentage function on a photocopier.

If the name is carved on a straight line it will look incongruous: square and bold. In order to be aesthetically pleasing the carved name must have a slight arch similar to, and certainly no more than, the crown of the transom.

Draw a curve on a piece of tracing paper and evenly space the letters along the curve. Turn the paper over and trace the letters through. Stick the tracing paper onto the transom with four pieces of masking tape. Spend a little time making sure that the name is in the right place. It must be central athwartships and the outside corners of the first and last letters must be the same distance from the waterline (if the transom is made of two or three boards it may be possible to measure down to a joint; alternatively level the boat up and use a spirit level).

The name ought to be above the half way point between the sculling notch and the waterline. Try to avoid any plugs on the centreline. Stand well back and have a look before tracing over the letters thus transferring the name to the transom.

Four chisels are needed for name carving. Two are standard flat chisels of ½in and ¼in; two were standard flat chisels of the same size and have been modified on a bench grinder to give a rounded end so that they can 'go round corners'. In order to do a crisp job the chisels must be really sharp. Start with a V cut in the centre of

25.1: Carving a stern board

25.2: Carving equipment

25.3: Chisel shapes

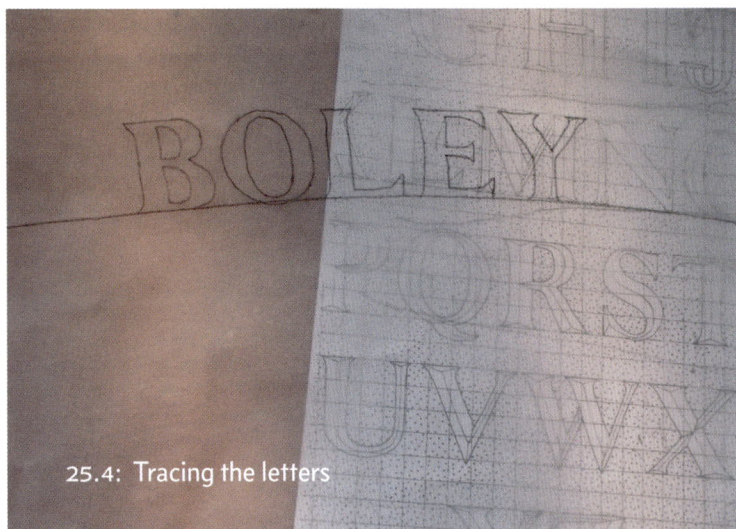

25.4: Tracing the letters

25.5: Transferring to the transom

25.6: Letters transferred onto transom (quite faint!)

25.7: V-cut to begin letter

25.8: Carving

25.9: A date

25.10: A complicated letter

25.11: Cove line end and carving at bow

25 Name carving

25.12: Gold leaf apparatus: gold size, 23.5 carat transfer leaf

25.13: Cove Line masked off

25.14: Applying transfer gold leaf and peeling off backing paper

25.15: Removing excess size with a thin rag and sharp-edged piece of wood

25.16: Gold leaf complete

the widest part of a letter. Extend the V cut over the letter so that the letter begins to appear.

Put the flat side of the curved chisel facing the wood that will remain to follow round a convex curve, and the rounded side facing the wood that will remain to follow round a concave curve.

Always cut out less than necessary to begin with. There will always be time to nibble out more wood. If you chomp too much away every letter will have to be swollen to cover the error. Having cut a few letters, stand back and check that the heights, depths and widths of the letters are uniform.

Once the whole name is carved pass your 'eye of uniformity' over the job again. By now you will be able to detect the smallest of irregularities. Words with the same letter side by side are the most awkward to carve.

There is no rush; however long the carving takes it will be there for the life of the boat and will draw the eye so it needs to look regular and crisp: in sum, professional.

Gold leaf

Gold leaf is microns thick. Boatbuilding work is diverse. If you have just been walloping a one-inch diameter bronze keel bolt with a 20lb maul through several tons of lead, have a cup of tea and prepare yourself for more delicate work.

Varnish the timber so that the pores are filled up. Apply the gold size (special glue) to the carving with a small paint brush. Make sure that all parts of the carving are well sized.

Size that has been applied outside the carving can be removed by putting a little white spirit on a thin rag, stretching it over a block of wood with a sharp edge and dragging this over the carving.

Wait until the size has become tacky like sellotape. Different sizes allow different time periods. A size that allows one hour should be fine for a name carving. One might allow a little longer for the Cutty Sark's cove line.

Carefully pick up a sheet of transfer gold leaf. Press it into the carving. Gold leaf will peel off the transfer paper and adhere to the size in the carving.

A stick equivalent to a blunt pencil is handy for pressing the transfer leaf into the sharp corners of the carving.

Once a letter has been inlaid with gold, dust over it with a small soft brush. This will remove any loose gold and also help to firmly bed the gold into the size.

Once all of the letters and carving are inlaid, using fine sand paper on a flat block, very lightly pass over the area a few times to remove any leaf that has adhered to the flat surface outside the letters, and particularly outside the more intricate carved flourishes.

The gold leaf work will have been done before the final coat of varnish. Although varnishing on top of the gold leaf will slightly diminish the lustre it will help it survive in the marine environment.

26 Oars

Spoon oars are a difficulty—an awful job because the blades are a sculpture for which there is little reference. Our standard dinghy oar size seems to be 8ft 6in; the loom is 1⅝in square. The timber is Oregon pine and the glue Resorcinol.

First glue up the blank; the loom should be made of two strips glued together. This creates a stronger loom that is less likely to bend, as by glueing two billets together there is inevitably some opposing grain. The glue joint should be vertical so that it creates a centreline, not lateral.

The blade is made from two pieces of the same cross section as the loom, glued onto the side of the loom. The two pieces should be one third the length of the loom.

Have an eye to the end grain on both the loom and the billets for the blade. It should be straight and perpedicular to the long dimension, which is also known as quarter sawn. When you shape the loom and blade the vertical grain will be easier to work and will also look uniform. Tiger grain on the front of a blade or loom looks scruffy.

Blade shaping

A little bollow plane is more or less essential to make the blade. First shape the hollow of the spoon. As it becomes deeper a central ridge needs to be carved in or rise out of the hollow. This central ridge starts at the neck and feathers away to nothing towards the lower end of the blade.

Once the hollow is shaped the back of the blade can be shaped. The excess timber is planed off the back to mirror the hollow on the front but tapering the thickness to ¼in at the sides and toe of the blade, whilst at the top of the blade on the back side the loom grows out of it. Clearly the blade wants to be as light as possible yet it needs to retain sufficient strength.

Loom shaping

The loom from the top of the leather to the blade is rounded, because it is easier to get a tight fit on the leather if it is sewn around a circle.

The loom is tapered slightly thwartships from the lower end of the leather to the top of the blade, but not in the fore and aft plane, as one does not want to take any strength out of the bite and pull of the blade. From the upper end of the leather to the handle the loom is left eight-sided. This is simply aesthetic.

To determine the start of the round loom, measure the beam of the dinghy and halve it. Measuring down from the end of the handle to the half beam of the dinghy, make a pencil mark on the oar. This is the centre of the leather. The leather is ten inches long therefore the rounding starts five inches inboard of the mark.

26.1: Glueing up the blanks

26.2: Glueing on the blades

Once the taper is cut the loom can be turned from four sides into eight. This is done with the ratio 7:10:7 marked across the flat. For this we have a spar gauge but it is equally well done with a ruler. Take off the new corners with a plane to turn the oar from eight sides to sixteen. This can probably be done by eye rather than marking up again. It is worth going close to your lines but do not go below the lines. It is also worth sighting along the planed lines every now and then to check that they are straight. Your eye will pick up minor deflections looking along a line with much greater ease than looking down upon a line.

At this point clamp the oar in a vice and with a long piece of sand paper turned so that the grit is facing inwards (a belt sander belt torn at the joint works well) sand off the high spots in a similar method as if you were drying your back with a towel (a nice soft one). The oar will have to be turned four times as each pass with the

26.3: Shaping the paddle

26.4: Shaping the paddle

26.5: Shaping the neck

26.6: Shaping the back

'towelling' method only fully fairs a quarter of a loom. This will make the loom almost round or smoothly oval as it goes down towards the blade.

Having completed the first pass put the sand paper down, grip the loom with your hand, close your eyes and feel the high spots on your palm. Touch down the high spots with a sharp block plane and feel the loom again. Even though the plane marks will be flats, you should be able to feel 'through' these and tell whether the loom is round or oval.

Use the sand paper towelling method again, perhaps with finer grit this time. On completion of the fourth pass things should be pretty fair. Sand along the grain by hand in order to remove the cross grain sanding marks. If you think they are all gone, wet the timber with white spirit to highlight any remaining marks.

To shape the handle, take the router bit used for the cove line and set the guide/fence at eight

143

26.7: Shaping the loom

26.8: Front of paddles complete

inches. This may involve a timber extension to the guide. Put the oar at an angle in a vice with the blade on the floor and the handle at chest height. With the guide/fence on the end of the handle run the router around the 8 sides. This gives a smooth termination to the handle and also gives a set depth for it. Round off to this depth. The handle is not varnished because bare wood promotes a firm grip.

If you are a really natty rower you will 'bounce' the handle ends together at each stroke.

A loose fitting canvas oar bag can be handy as it as it prevents the oars clattering about on the varnish when transporting the dinghy.

27 Waterline

By painting one colour below the waterline and either varnishing or painting another colour above, the boat will appear sleeker. The difficulty lies in marking a straight line on a surface of compound curves.

Determine the waterline at stem and transom (either from the plans, or drop the boat in the water, have a heavy friend relax on the central thwart and whilst wearing a long pair of wellies make the two marks with a pencil). It will look smarter if the waterline shows when the boat is afloat so when back in the shed lift the marks up ½in at both stem and transom, mark with a pencil and rub out the lower marks to avoid confusion.

Sand the planking so that it is ready for finishing. Use a spinning laser level if available. The job is quick and easy. If a spinning laser level is not to hand turn the dinghy upside down and level it in both directions. Attach horizontal battens to the stem and stern posts with the top edge of the batten on the pencil mark (as shown in the photographs). The battens must be straight and horizontal and may need 'legs' to hold them in position.

Sight across the two battens to check that they are not twisted: with one eye open visually lower the further batten onto the nearer batten making sure that, along its length, the further batten is eclipsed at the same moment.

Also check that the 'eclipse' happens at the same point midships on both sides of the boat as you don't want the waterline to be higher on one side than the other. The waterline is now ready to be marked.

One person crouches down and sights across the battens, the other follows the instructions of 'up' or 'down' until the sharp point of the pencil is in line with the moment of eclipse of the further batten. A pencil mark is made. A mark every six inches is adequate, more may be needed towards the ends of the boat. Sighting through can only be done from one end to midships, then change end or side. Some scribe the line with a batten and the edge of a sharp chisel. We do that on bigger boats but not on dinghies.

If you want a boot top as well use battens that are the thickness of the boot top (perhaps an inch) and sight both underneath and over the top. Don't be alarmed when the boot top appears to get wider towards the transom where the planking is more horizontal than vertical.

Finishing products should be single-pack and oil based. It is not good for the longevity of a timber vessel to paint with epoxy or two-part paints. This mixes an organic material with a plastic and may lead to tears in the future.

Unless a dinghy is to stay afloat in salt water long term she need not be antifouled. A standard

27.1: Setting up for the waterline

27.2: Setting up for the waterline

27.3: Setting up for the waterline

27.4: Masking the waterline

27 Waterline

gloss paint underwater works very well. Any dirt or minor growth simply washes or wipes off, and when wrestling with the dinghy there is no mess on clothes from an ablating antifoul. A light colour will reflect heat and be kinder to the planking; a dark colour will absorb heat.

I dimly design to remember the man who flew in the face of all recommendations, assuring us of his superior knowledge when insisting on black antifoul underneath his new dinghy which he then parked outside on concrete. His subsequent complaints were not well received.

Put a coat of thinned varnish on the outside of the boat. This will seal the marks in place. Put ten coats of varnish on the topsides and this can come down a little past the water line in order that the paint overlaps the varnish and properly seals the timber.

Mask off the waterline. In order to get the saw-tooth effect on the underside of the clinker

27.5: Sawtooth masking

27.6: Painting below the waterline

27.7: Painting below the waterline

planking, mask along the lower plank in a fair line and then with a Stanley knife, cut back to the edge of the plank above.

Paint the colour under the waterline. Be sure to tape a covering skirt over the newly completed varnish. If this is thought to be an effort too far, consider how long it will take to re-varnish when many little spots of paint have flicked un-noticed onto the varnish. This is another bad memory of the working struggle.

Then re-mask both the lower and upper edge of the boot top and paint the boot top.

Be careful not to pull any paint off when removing the masking tape if the underwater paint is still green. If there is creep under the masking tape rub off with a flat head screwdriver pushed inside a rag dipped in white spirit.

Once the external hull is finished, work can start on the capping, sheer and interior varnish as required.

27.8: Masking the boot top

27.9: Sawtooth waterline and boot top masked off at stern

27.10: Masking the boot top

27.11: Paint below the waterline

The quality of paint and varnish work is open ended; it can simply get better and better until it is perfect and then she will need another coat of varnish after her maiden voyage anyway. Some enjoy aiming for a perfect finish and others prefer to spend time afloat. Whilst the planks have to fit perfectly whatever finish will be applied, the finishing can be completed to personal taste.

One thought before you finish her with Stockholm tar on the topside and tallow underwater: the casual bystander looks at the paint job and bases any conclusions in respect of quality of work upon the finish. Perfect paint has been the basis of much mis-judgement with regard to wooden boats. Cleanliness and carefulness should be the maxims of a good finisher.

28 Rubbing bands

The keel band is convex ⅝in brass strip. It starts at the stem head, runs along the keel and ends on the transom. The bilge runners also have brass strip in order to protect them from chafe. Cut the brass to length for the bilge runners and round off the ends. Offer up and mark where the copper nail heads are in order to avoid them. Drill 4mm holes through the brass and countersink accordingly. Fasten with 6G by ¾in counter sunk bronze wood screws.

The keel band is a little more tricky as it is liable to break on the tight curve of the forefoot or skeg. Fit in two pieces (brass convex is sold in ten-foot lengths). Grind and polish a suitable ending onto the brass. On the bench drill the holes along the part that will be flat on the keel. Drill one hole one inch below the end on the stem piece and do the same on the transom piece. At this stage do not drill any holes where the brass has to bend as it will snap on the hole rather than bend. Fasten in position on the flat of the keel.

Maintaining a supporting pressure on the worst of the bend, pull the brass tightly around the forefoot and get the top fastening in. It is important to pull the brass tightly around the bend. Centrepunch and drill the holes between the flat part of the keel and the ending. To avoid drilling great clearance holes in the stem when you burst through the brass, put a hacksaw blade behind the hole. Repeat the process at the stern.

28.1: Marking the bilge rubber brass to avoid fastenings

28.2: Centre-punching and drilling brass

28.3: Supporting the brass band and bending around the skeg

28.4: Drilling brass on stem with hacksaw blade

28.5: Brass bands fitted

29 Sailing dinghy backbone

The sailing dinghy backbone is similar in construction to the standard rowing dinghy backbone with one exception. Rather than having a parallel width of keel at 1⅛in like the rowing dinghy, the sailing dinghy has a shaped keel to allow for the centreboard slot.

Cut out all of the backbone members to the full size plan templates in preparation for assembly of the backbone. The skeg and forefoot pieces can have an initial fore and aft taper.

The forward end of the skeg will be the width of the central slotted section and the aft end the width of the stern post. It is best to give this taper some curve (like a fine cigar) rather than making it straight as a little bit of timber left on is something to adjust later on. The forefoot piece will be the width of the stem forward and the width of the central slotted section aft.

The backbone is built from aft to forward in a similar manner to the rowing dinghy: The sternpost is tenoned into the skeg; the hog is steamed onto the skeg; the forward end of the hog is steamed and the forefoot piece used as a shape former (this can remain temporarily clamped in position).

The stern knee and transom are fitted; the stern assembly is turned upside down and attached to the moulds and building frame; the forefoot piece is temporarily unclamped; the slotted central section is fitted to the skeg scarph; the forefoot piece is fitted to the slotted central section; the forward end of the hog is cut off flush with the end of the forefoot piece; the stem is fitted; and finally the stem knee is fitted.

There are two differences in the pattern of construction: Unlike the rowing dinghy, the stem, forefoot piece and stem knee are not assembled as a unit and then attached to the dinghy. They are attached to the backbone assembly individually; unlike the rowing dinghy the forward end of the hog has a bend in it to follow the line of the rabbet--this has to be steamed into the curve of the forefoot piece.

Measure the length of the hog reasonably accurately on the drawing and add say four inches. Check this measurement over the building moulds. Steam the forward end of the hog for say two feet and clamp the forefoot piece on as a former. This can stay in position until the slotted central section of the keel is attached to the backbone.

When fitting the forefoot piece to the backbone, lay your hands on a reliable and strong straightedge. A piece of aluminium box section or C channel is great or a length of straight timber perfectly adequate. Clamp the straightedge on top of the keel once the forefoot piece is in position. Wind the clamps up until the straightedge

29.1: Sailing dinghy backbone components, from the bow

29.2: Stern components of the sailing dinghy backbone

29.3: Sailing dinghy keel with centreboard slot and 'bridge'

29.4: Tapering the skeg

29.5: Sternpost fitted to tapered skeg

29.6: Preparing the forefoot piece scarph

29.7: Dry fitting the stem to forefoot piece scarph

29 Sailing dinghy backbone

29.8: Steaming the forward end of the hog

29.9: Dry fitting the stem to forefoot piece

29.10: Clamping the forefoot piece and stem into position

29.11: Faired backbone ready for stopwaters and rabbet

29.12: Faired backbone showing sweep of the sides of the keel and tapered skeg

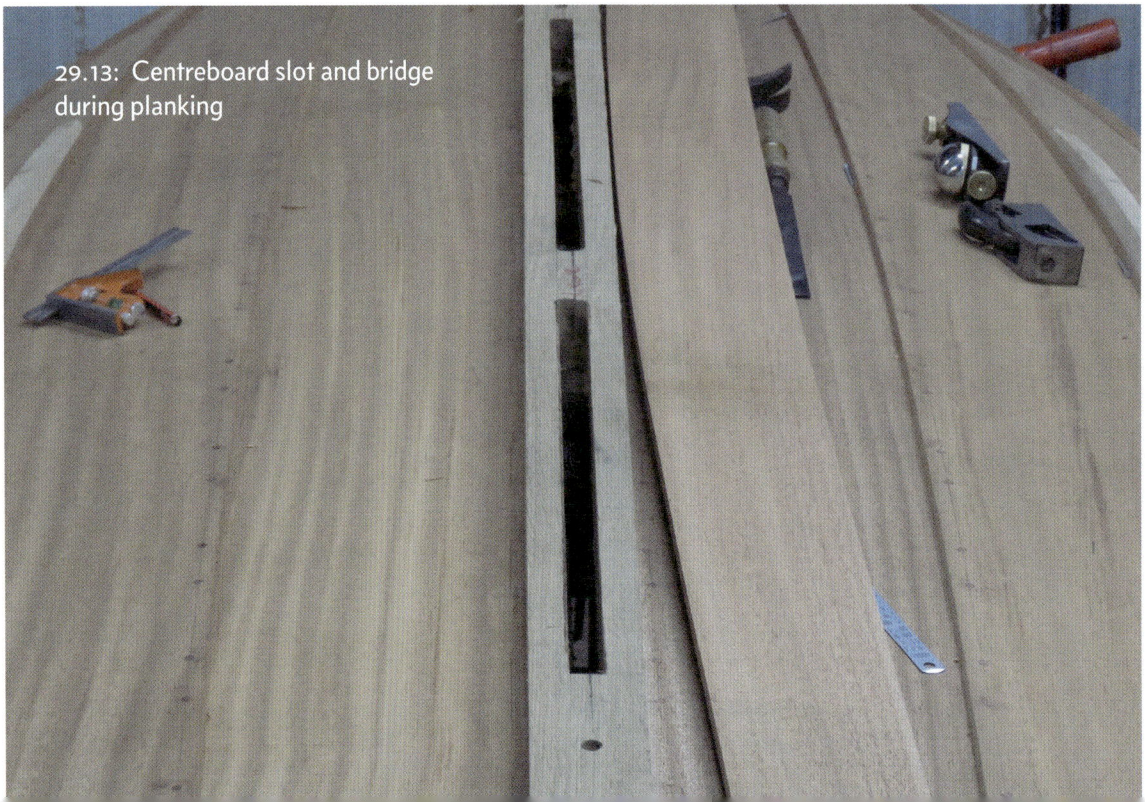

29.13: Centreboard slot and bridge during planking

is touching the keel and the hog is home in the forefoot piece. In the worst case the forward end of the hog may need another fifteen minutes of steam.

Mark any small adjustments to the scarph between forefoot piece and the central slotted section of the keel, remove the forefoot piece, fettle and refit.

All backbone members are glued together with Gorilla glue or similar as for the rowing dinghy. The backbone is fastened as in a rowing dinghy with the exception of the central slotted section. There are no fastenings either side of the centre board slot as these fastenings are put in when the centre case is fitted. There is another thing to bear in mind: if the central section has a slot all the way along, the slot is liable to be compressed when fitting the garboards. Leave a 'bridge' in the slot for say three inches midships. This will outwit the lateral forces of compression.

The hog slot can be cut out from above once the planking has been completed and the dinghy turned over. Drill a hole up through the slot from underneath either side of the bridge. From above use a straight and parallel sided router cutter with a bottom bearing in a palm router. Square out the corners by hand. The bridge will be cut out later.

Before cutting the rabbet, the backbone should be faired. Bear in mind that it will not be a single shallow curve on either side of the keel. It is more likely to be a very shallow or flattened sombrero. The central part of the keel with the slot has more or less parallel sides in way of the slot and then begins to taper through the scarphs onto the forefoot piece forward and the skeg aft.

Don't forget to vertically taper the skeg a little at its aft end, otherwise it may look heavy and rather like a lump of wood. The stem will be bearded in due course and this tapering will flow into the forefoot piece. Even though the sweep of the keel may have minor concavity at either end of the central slotted section, the curve must be fair; we don't want the fish thinking we have lost the touch.

30 Centreboard case

Centreboard cases are notorious for leaking, either because the joints are not waterproof or because they flex and pant at the connection to the boat when the dinghy is heeled, with lateral water pressure on the centreboard acting as a lever upon the centre case. These leaks need to be 'headed off at the pass' in two stages. The first stage is the construction of the box itself. The second stage is the integration of the box into the dinghy's structure.

It would be rare to find a timber board wide enough and free from defects for the centre board casing. More often than not two planks need to be jointed and glued together with a loose tongue. Once the two side boards of the casing have been made, they need to be connected together with a spacer to make the centre-case box.

A little space either side of the plate gives reduced chance of a jam and a little wiggle room (though this may be poor advice for a pure racing dinghy). The plate will be ¼in brass. With ¼in either side of the plate the internal slot of the centre-case will be ¾in.

A spacer 1in fore and aft and ¾in wide is machined and then a ¼in deep groove cut (either with a table saw or better a rebating router cutter) down the centre of either 1in face. A corresponding groove is cut in the inside face of each end of the centre case boards. A degree of accuracy is needed at this point: the middle of that groove will be ½in forward of the fore end of the centreboard slot in the keel and ½in aft of its aft end. This means that the aft face of the forward spacer will be in column with the fore end of the keel slot and the forward face of the aft spacer will be in column with the aft face of the keel slot; the reason will become apparent below when the casing is installed.

Once the assembly has been dry fitted with the loose tongues, all is glued and clamped together. Once the glue has cured the cramps can be removed and screws put through the side of the centreboard casing into the spacer. Make sure that the screws are staggered port and starboard otherwise they will hit each other.

Flush and square off the casing boards' top and bottom edges, the spacer, and the end cappings. Whilst it is simpler if the case is straight, it doesn't matter if the box has a small bow because it will be 'bent straight' at installation.

Forward and aft cappings are then fitted, glued and screwed into the end grain of the casing side boards. A stopped staff bead can be run up the end capping, or a simple stop chamfer, depending on your tastes. The box itself is now made and can be expected to be water tight.

The box needs a pair of legs in order to engage with the keel. Cut three timbers ¾in

30.1: Groove in the centrecase boards for the spacer tongue

30.2: Glueing and clamping the box together

30.3: Cleaning off the ends and screwing the box together

30.4: Fitting the end capping

square and as long as the distance from the top of the casing to the base of the keel, plus some spare. When machining small pieces it is good to have six inches spare at either end as there is often machining damage in the ends. Tap two of the timbers into position at either end of the case. They want to be a gentle drive fit, be close up against the spacer at either end, and flush with the top of the casing. Wind a pair of screws staggered in from either side to hold them in position.

Tap the third timber down the centre of the casing as a temporary spacer to ensure a uniform ¾in gap and to take any bow out of the casing when it is dry fitted.

Lower the centreboard casing into place; the legs will locate it fore and aft and ensure it is not listing; its base will now be resting on the timbers. Scribe the timbers using the base of the casing as a guide line; remove the casing and cut the timbers immediately inboard of the scribed line.

30.5: Close-up of the joints

30.6: Centreboard casing with capping and staff bead

30.7: Screwing the case into the boat in an early build; it has since been found easier to fit the casing when the hull planking is complete

30.8: Fitting the thwart

30 Centreboard case

Tap the casing back into position in order to drill for the fastenings; settle down underneath the dinghy and prepare to get drill swarf in the face; counterbore and clearance drill the keel then pilot hole the centreboard casing.

Remove the casing, clean away all the drill swarf, spread some glue on the casing, legs and keel faying faces, re-fit and wind the screws in tightly from below so that the casing is pulled firmly onto the keel all the way along.

The thwart which crosses the centre case will both brace it and ensure that the slot space is even. It will also give compression for the keel. The main casing thwart is fitted with some crown; this means that the top of the centre case is say ¼in higher than the rising.

Mark the centreline of the thwart. On either side and ⅜in clear of the centreline, cut a groove ¾in wide and ⅜in deep. These slots will engage with the top of the centre case,

30.9: Close-up of the thwart joint

30.10: Fitting the knees

30.11: Fitting the cappings

30.12: Fitting the cappings

ensuring that it cannot move laterally. The ¾in wide piece left in between the slots will ensure that the top of the casing is the same width as the base. The forward thwart just engages with the forward end of the casing acting as a further thwartship brace.

Cappings are fitted to close the casing aft of the main thwart and bring this open part up to the level of the thwarts. Knees are fitted underneath the centre casing thwarts to further prevent twist. These are straight grain timbers shaped to look in keeping with the other knees. They are glued and screwed rather than riveted. The crown in the thwart will ensure that the keel is under compression preventing backbone hog in the future.

The central piece of timber left in the wood keel to prevent the planking process twisting or compressing the slot can now be sawn out of the wood keel from underneath.

31 Centreplate

The centreplate is made of ¼in brass and cut out to the template with a jigsaw or grinder. The top handle or horn can be left at a single thickness but is a bit prettier and more comfortable to grip in the event of a jam if it is a bit thicker. To make it thicker, rivet a ⅛in piece of copper to either side of it. Dress the rivets into countersinks in the copper and polish off flush, and smooth off all sharp edges.

The centreplate bolt is another leaking rogue. The following describes a system which allows the bolt to be tightened so that it will not leak, yet the tightening does not compress the centre case slot

Cut a bush from bronze rod; the ideal stock is an old piece of prop shaft of say 1in diameter. Cut off a ¾in long piece and drill a 10mm hole through the centre of the rod. The ends do need to be square.

Cut a hole in the centreplate at the pivot point (taken from the plans) that is the outside diameter of the bush. Drill a 9.5mm hole through the centre case at the pivot point. Make sure the drill is square to the centreline fore and aft and horizontal otherwise your centreplate will not be vertical.

As a general rule for all boat building only used shanked bolts – do not use fully threaded bolts. Put the bush in the centreplate and lower the centreplate into position. At this stage a helper is ideal – after many frustrations there will be light right through the pivot hole. At this moment the plate holder must hold steady and the ⅜in bolt can be driven right through. Following words of mutual congratulation (kind words go a long way) the washer and nut can be wound on and the bolt done up tight. The bolt is compressing the centre casing against the ends of the bush. It will not leak nor can the casing be compressed. The centreplate is free to rotate on the bush and will fall into the lowered position under its own weight. In order to raise it a luff tackle is used.

An eye plate is attached to the underside of the aft deck beam and a single block with becket is shackled to it; a single block is shackled to the plate horn. The rope is rove with a dead end spliced onto the becket, around the sheave on the centreplate, back around the sheave on the deck beam eye plate, and the fall comes to the starboard aft end of the centre casing where it can be reached when sailing.

In order to prevent damage to the timber fit a 1in length of either the ⅛in copper or the centreplate brass into the top at either end of the centre case. The plate horn will knock against this when pulled up or let down. This also gives a satisfying and confirmatory 'clack' sound.

31.1: Bush and pivot bolt

31.2: Horn with copper cheeks

31.3: Centreplate pulled up

32 Rudder

The rudder – the lever by which you steer – is good fun to make. Cut out the parts as per the full size patterns. This will give you two cheeks and a central billet for the stock and a blade.

Concentrating first on the stock, the two cheeks are riveted together with the central billet sandwiched in between. A socket is left for the tiller. This socket is parallel sided and the width of the central billet but it is a little tapered fore and aft. The taper is on the lower side of the chock that goes above the tiller socket. The blade of the rudder, where it is hidden between the rudder stock cheeks, is ¾in thick. From the base of this circle to the lower tip of the rudder, the blade is tapered.

There is a step on the fore-edge of the rudder and this corresponds with a step on the billet between the rudder stock cheeks; this prevents the rudder blade from going any further forward than vertical. An early dinghy suffered an unseen problem of minor magnitude when she would not answer her helm. The rudder had jammed because it had gone forward of vertical and fouled the skeg.

In order to make things easy later on (it is a case of deferred gratification as it is a bit more tricky initially) lead can be riveted into the rudder blade to make it self- lowering. Three weights are generally enough; drill holes with a hole saw through the blade that are the same size as the circles of lead you plan to fit; chamfer both sides of these holes; clamp timber across the blade to prevent the blade splitting up the grain and very gently rivet the lead into the holes. Gentleness is needed as rivets have great power of expansion and have split a blade beyond repair when riveting in a lead weight. Once the countersinks have been filled, the remaining lead can be shorn off with an electric planer and then a belt sander. Lead fitted, hold an old bolt through the pivot hole and take the blade down to the water's edge. With the pivot hole just above water level the blade should sink down to a vertical position. If this does not happen a fourth piece will be required.

When sailing and the rudder be raised from the 'deep beneath' in a hurry, the blade can break out the end grain of the central billet. The remedy is to put a thick copper nail (we use ⅜in bar) through the cheeks just as the central billet comes to nothing aft.

A 2in x ⅝in piece of brass convex (which is an offcut from the bilge runner brass) is let into the corresponding part of the blade edge. This gives a satisfying clack when raised with the added cheer that no varnish has been damaged. An up-haul is spliced through a hole

32.1: Marking out the pattern

32.2: Full size yard templates

32.3: Cutting out the stock

32.4: Assembling the stock

⅔ of the way down the aft edge of the blade. A splice on the upper end is loosely hooked over a small cleat on the aft face of the stock. To raise the blade, haul in mightily on the thick cable and belay handsomely on the huge cleat.

The rudder blade is secured between the cheeks of the stock in a similar manner to the centreplate in the centre case. A small bush is cut which is fitted in the pivot point of the blade. When aligned with the pivot hole through the cheeks of the stock, this is all through-bolted with a ⅜in bronze cup square bolt. This allows the cheeks to be bolted firmly together without clamping them onto the blade. Whether you have the nut to port or starboard will signify to those in the know whether you are Cornish or from Devon; in operational terms it is neither here nor there.

The rudder is positioned on the transom so that the tiller is clear to work under the horse and

32.5: Rivets all on one side

32.6: Drilling square for the pivot bolt

32.7: Riveting in the lead

the base of the stock is above the height of the keel when the blade is up.

The lower pintle on the transom is the long one and the upper pintle on the rudder the short one. This is so that you can engage one pintle at a time, and the lower one first. Offer up the rudder hangings to the rudder and transom, hold them in place with masking tape and mark where they are to be fitted. Permanently fit the hangings to the rudder first. It may be that you have to clip off the end of the screws fastening the lower gudgeon to the rudder as they do not want to protrude into the blade bay. Offer up to the transom again, making any small adjustments necessary for the siting of the transom hangings prior to fastening the transom hangings.

The tiller is made of ash; it wants to be a neat fit in the rudder stock but not so tight that it has to be driven into position; before going to sea it can be rubbed with a candle. The aft end

32.8: Template detail of the rudder stop when deployed

32.9: Bush and shanked bolt for the pivot

32.10: Detail of the uphaul stop

32.11: Lower pintle and gudgeon

of the tiller has a taper to suit the rudder stock and should protrude beyond the rudder stock by say ½in; its ends should be neatly chamfered. The sides of the tiller have shoulders that butt up against the rudder stock but the top and the bottom of the tiller do not have shoulders, being the same width as the tiller heel. Once the tiller is fitted, a hole is drilled through the centre of the tiller heel aperture in the rudder stock and countersunk either side. We are lucky to have a hessian sack of pre-war short ⅜in countersunk copper rivets which seem to be perfect tiller pins. As these are a finite resource, it is worth tying the tiller pin onto the upper rudder pintle. The tiller itself can be shaped to suit and the length is arbitrary.

32.12: Tiller detail

32.13: Tiller pin and uphaul cleat

32.14: Dis-assembled rudder

32.15: Assembled rudder

32 Rudder

32.16: Mini-rudder for a ten-foot dinghy

33 Deck beams

Deck beams want to be close enough together so there is no flex in the deck yet far enough apart so weight is kept to a minimum. A rule of thumb for deck beam crown is ⅜in to ½in amidships per foot of beam. For a dinghy, while the beams will be tapered, it is simplest to cut the beams out of the timber stock parallel; this also means that they can be nested on the timber stock with a minimum of cuts.

Fit the beams square to the gunwale top; there is no need to fit them with a plumb or vertical face – this is only beneficial in boats with bulkheads. Mark the beam positions square to the centreline. Presuming your ship is more or less the same both sides, this can be done by measuring an equal distance port and starboard in a straight line from the centre of the stemhead.

Lay your beam (initially a bit too long) across the boat with say the aft face on both the port and starboard gunwale marks, mark the position of the beam and angle it makes with the gunwale on the top of the gunwale and then square down the inboard face of the gunwale.

Cut the dovetails on one side of the beam only – either aft or forward; leave the other side full. Cut the dovetail on the beam first, lay the beam in position and scribe the tail onto the gunwale. Cut the dovetails to half the depth of the gunwale; it is a shame to cut into the gunwale at all but in these circumstances, what can a boatbuilder do? Cut the gunwale just inside the scribed line as this wants to be a tap home fit. Measuring half the gunwale depth down from the top of the beam, cut off the base of the dovetail; the shoulder may have a small bevel if the gunwale is not vertical at the beam position.

When dry fitting, mark the beams for tapering on their underside; the lower outboard edge of the beam will meet the top of the beading on the gunwale. Remove the beam and cramp a batten onto it, leaving the beam full midships and tapered towards the marks on the outboard ends. Scribe the line at the underside of the batten and cut to the line. Chamfer the underside of the beam with a stop chamfer. If using a palm router, the edge of the router base provides a uniform stop distance when it reaches the end of the beam.

Fasten the dove tail into the beam with a 1in x 10G bronze gripfast nail, countersunk just below flush so that there is scope for fairing. Inevitably some fairing will be needed on the top of the beams although hopefully this will be minimal. For fairing, use a stiff batten; press it down lightly and it should touch all of the beams. Plane down any proud beams; start on the centreline and work outboard. Whilst the batten is always fore and aft, make sure the beams also remain fair athwartships during your fairing

33 Deck beams

33.1: Laying the beams in position

33.2: Marking the dovetail on the gunwale on a side deck

33.3: Dovetail tapped home

33.4: Marking the taper

33.5: Beam tapered and ready to fit

33.6: Deck beams fitted and ready for fairing

33.7: Fairing the deck with a stiff batten

34 Deck

Make the deck from two layers of ³⁄₁₆in mahogany; hopefully these can be machined out of planking offcuts. The width of the planks is arbitrary and could be between four and six inches; perhaps five might be a happy medium. Fit the deck before the gunwale capping; overlap it onto half of the gunwale in order to support the tapered plank ends.

The first, central plank of the lower layer will establish all the plank seams parallel with the centreline fore and aft. Mark a centreline on the aft face of the stem, on the aft six inches of the underside of the first plank, and on the aft face of the aft deck beam. Cut the forward end of the first plank of the lower layer, line up its centreline with the marks, and tack it in position with brass panel pins; leave the aft end overhanging the beam for now. Fit the remaining first layer planks port and starboard working out from the central plank. Tack them into position with brass panel pins; the seams should be barely visible later on. Cut the first layer off flush with the aft face of the aft deck beam.

Draw a new centreline down the central plank using the mark on the aft face of the stem and on the aft face of the aft deck beam as pick up points. Fit the second layer over the first layer with the seams staggered, so that a seam between two boards in the upper layer is above the middle of a lower lay board. Fit the second layer boards either side of the recently drawn centreline. Dry fit the whole of the second layer without fastening it down. For ease of keeping things in place, you can tack it temporarily in position with panel pins. These should just enter the lower layer so that they can be pulled out later. These pins can be put in the planks above the beams and say ¾in from the plank edge.

Fix the second layer to the first using epoxy glue; this has a reasonable working time, which should avoid a glue panic. Start with one of the pair of central planks; glue both the upper face of the lower layer and the lower face of the upper layer. Use enough glue so that the timber is not dry but not so much that the two pieces of timber cannot come together. Tack the pieces in place with the panel pins as before – perhaps set in slightly further but still removable when the glue has cured; this will all be a bit messy.

Once all of the planks are glued and in place clamp the whole second layer into place with battens across the deck; the clamps can hook under the edge of the sheer plank. Don't just hook under the rubbing band as you might make it unfair; you won't shift the sheer plank though. It might be a consideration to put some small pads underneath the clamp foot to spread the pressure a bit.

34.1: Fitting the lower layer

34.2: Lower layer complete

Once the glue has cured, approximately twenty-four hours later, cut the aft end of the second layer flush with the aft face of the deck beam; sand the deck fair.

Once the deck is fair it can be connected to the deck beams using 12G x 1in bronze gripfast nails. If you can reach in and support the beams from below with a lump hammer before thumping in the gripfast nails it will be a better job. Make sure that you drill both pilot and clearance holes, and to make a small countersink in the deck so that the nail head does not crush the surrounding timber. Ensure the countersink is not so large that it can be seen around the nail head.

Using a combination set square adjusted to reach from the outboard edge of the rubbing band to half way across the gunwale, scribe a line on the top edge of the deck, and cut it carefully with a small circular saw set to a depth a little less than the deck thickness. Clean up the cut

34.3: Clamping on the upper layer

34.4: Trimming the deck edge

34.5: Cutting the rebate

edge with a rebate plane. Setting the set square to reach to the inboard edge of the capping (overlaps the inboard edge of the gunwale by ⅛in) scribe another line on the deck. Set the circular saw to a little less than half the deck thickness and cut to the outside of this line. Clean it up with a rebate plane.

Make a corresponding rebate in the lower inboard edge of the ⅜in capping. Glue the capping on with an epoxy glue and screw it down to the gunwale and sheer plank edge as the standard capping aft. With the capping done, fit a shedwater at the aft end of the foredeck; this covers the end grain of the deck, and will be approximately ¾in thick. Glue and screw it to the aft face of the deck beam; you don't want water penetrating this joint, wicking up the deck end grain, and causing decay. Make a plywood pattern of the forward edge of the shedwater and consider the increasing bevels of the shedwater at the gunwales.

34.6: Fastening the capping

34.7: Fairing and plugging the capping

34.8: Deck faired and fastened

34.9: Patterning the shedwater

34.10: Patterning the shedwater

34.11: Deck complete

35 Mast step and partners

The mast step locates the mast heel; it is made of oak. Ideally the central section is rectangular and the fore and aft sections are tapered athwartships and vertically. It then looks well-made rather than like a lump of wood. The tenon at the mast heel is not parallel sided but shaped as a trapezium so that that mast can only be put up the right way; the mortise in the step is correspondingly shaped. The step has two lateral 10G rivets, one forward and one aft of the mortise; this stops any possibility of it breaking out athwartships. Due to the leverage of the mast, there can be a lot of lateral pressure on the step when sailing to windward.

Ideally the mast step is set down on top of the frames. Small rebates or channels ¼in deep are cut into the base of the step so that it locates over the steamed timbers. This ensures the compression of the mast is spread up the timbers and the side of the boat rather than being a point loading on the hog and keel. If the mast step is set down snug on the hog then a gap has to be cut below the mast heel to prevent the mast step becoming a water trap. It is best to set the mast step down on the frames because over time point loading may cause the garboards to leak in way of the mast. This is less likely on a lug rig without stays.

The mast step is riveted through the keel with 8G copper nails. These can either be through a timber or adjacent to a timber. It is possible that over time a larger hole through a timber would cause it to crack.

If fastening through a timber, remove the existing nail by carefully cutting the copper poking through the rivet off with an angle grinder and knocking the nail out. Drill up through the existing hole. The nail comes up from underneath the keel, its head in a counter-bore under the keel, and the rivet is made up on the mast step top face. If fastening adjacent to the timbers, packers are fitted beside each frame and between the mast step and hog, say one inch fore and aft width and spanning the width of the hog. The rivets are set through these packers.

A bronze ⅜in eyebolt goes through the step abaft the mast. The boom downhaul block is shackled to it, the rope being attached to the boom, rove through the block and made off on one of the belaying pins in the mast partners. Countersinking the nut of this bolt into the base of the keel would mean removing quite a lot of keel timber. To avoid this the nut is fitted via a hole in the side of the keel to the 'galleried bolt'.

Drill down from above into the keel to a depth say ¾in below the garboard. Noting where this hole is in relation to the surrounding copper nails, find the location outside the boat on the side of the keel. With a small bit, drill gently into the

35.1: Mast step shape

35.2: Mast step joggles

35.3: Mast step with through rivets and drainage under the heel

35.4: Mast partner

side of the keel ½in below the garboard and you will discover the void. Open this hole out with a chisel until the nut and a washer can be slid into it and lined up with the thread of the bolt from above. Cut any excess thread off the bolt; always wind the nut onto the bolt before doing so as then when you wind the nut off the bolt you clear out any damage to the cut thread end. Having popped the nut and washer into the gallery, and preventing the nut from spinning with a screwdriver, wind the bolt down into the nut. It is best if the bolt hole goes a little below the nut so that should the bolt be a little long it can be wound down tight without bottoming out. Fill the gallery hole with a chock of timber and keep the secret.

The mast partners are fitted to the aft face of the shedwater, which is itself fastened to the aft face of the aft deck beam. The partners have an octagonal hole into which the lower section of the mast fits snugly and without wedges. The

35.5: Mast partners and knees

35.6: Mast partner copper and belaying pins

35.7: Mast fitted snugly in the partners

35.8: Centreplate uphaul eye

edges of the octagonal hole are chamfered so that there is no sharp edge on the lead in. The mast partner is scarphed into a lodging knee port and starboard which prevents twist. An additional hanging knee can be fitted port and starboard under the deck beam if very serious sailing is to be undertaken. The partner and the lodging knee are riveted through the deck beam. A copper plate is cut and riveted over the mast partner in order to back up the short grain. The copper nails are set into the timber from underneath and riveted into a countersunk hole on the top of the plate. The excess is sanded off to make the fastenings all but invisible. The two ½in belaying pins sit in holes drilled through the copper. It is worth countersinking these holes so there is no sharp edge. A small eye plate is screwed underneath the mast partner, port or starboard of the mast, to taste. This plate takes the forward end of the centreplate uphaul tackle

36 Mainsheet horse

Most of the dinghy fittings are 'off the shelf' items. The horse is a little more complicated and has to be made for the boat. It is a satisfying minor engineering task.

After having bent a horse – no pun springs immediately to mind – when sailing, we make things a little on the heavy side so that there is confidence in the gear. The horse is made from ½in brass bar. It is fitted so that it can be easily removed should the helmsman want to take up the scull. When taking the measurements allow excess on the legs as this can always be cut off later.

There are two sets of stops: those that are on the cross bar which prevent the traveller jamming on the corners and those that are on the quarter knees which determine the height of the horse above the tiller. The stops are made from 1in diameter bar; ½in long and with a 13mm hole; they are held in place with grub screws.

The traveller is made on a lathe. It is made from 1in round bar or (1¼in if you would like a central boss) and is 2in long. A ⅜in bronze shackle is opened out and bolted onto it. Remember to slide the traveller and traveller stops onto the bar before it is bent in the pipe bender. Failure to do so will mean that you go round the bend trying to get the traveller and stops around the bend.

We use a pipe bender to shape the horse. The crown of the horse should be a little less than the crown of the transom. There should be up to five inches of clearance between the top of the transom and the horse.

A pair of rowlock plates are let into the transom knees so that the stops bear on metal and don't damage the timber. The stops may have to have a bevelled underside in order to neatly fit against the rowlock plates. A pair of timber chocks (similar to rowlock chocks) are riveted onto the transom with 10G nails. Dry fit the horse and mark the brass bar at the underside of these chocks.

Remove the horse and mark ¾in below the mark made. Cut off the excess brass bar, put a small bevel on the end to help the die get a grip, and thread the bar with a ½in UNC hand die for 1in (to a point ½in above the mark made). Fit a washer and dome nut.

With regard to the fittings in general: before fastening, it is important to put the fittings in place and step back to look at them from different angles to check that they look right. Raised head countersunk crews can be more attractive than flat head countersunk screws.

36 Mainsheet horse

36.1: Traveller and stops

36.3: Horse shaped with extra length in the legs

36.2: Measuring the bar and pipe bender

36.4: Dry fitting the horse

36.5: Horse fitted

36.6: Rowlock plate on the quarter knee

37 Leather work

Leather work is great fun because by this stage in the job all the worry is behind you. The oars and yard will have leather sewn onto them. It seems the best stuff for the job is 3mm natural veg tan leather. A set of sail maker's needles are needed and some heavy duty whipping twine. We haven't graduated to bent needles yet.

Measure across the rowlocks and divide the measurement in half. This half beam distance will be the position of the middle of the leather from the tip of the oar handle. The oar leather is ten inches long. It could be sewn with the stitching facing upwards in the rowlock so it will not chafe. This would be parallel with the blade. However, this would mean that the oars are handed which can be a hassle. We simply sew the seam in line with the middle of the blade so either oar can be used on either side. The seam faces aft which is the point of minimum pressure in the rowlock.

Seam chafe is of course foremost in one's mind when desperately rowing as George Orwell found with his 3 year old son aboard when escaping from the whirlpool in the Gulf of Corryvrecan.

In order to find the position of the leather on the yard simply raise the yard un-leathered or even better go for a sail with the yard un-leathered. The small area of chafe will tell you where the middle of the leather needs to be. The yard leather can be up to thirty inches long.

Make a pattern of the area to be leathered from thick paper. Cut off a one-inch strip of leather and bend it around the oar or yard – make a mark where the leather overlaps itself. Check this distance against your template to see if the template is giving a true reading. Adjust the template accordingly. Cut out the leather using a steel rule or piece of timber as a straight edge – please be careful not to cut yourself! Once the leather is cut out pop it into a bucket of water with a weight on top to keep it submerged.

A few hours later or the next day take the leather out of the water and stretch it around the job. Cut off any excess so that the two edges meet. Lay the leather down flat and mark a line ¼in in from the two meeting edges. For the oar leather, drill a 3mm hole every ½in along the length having started ¼in from each end. For the yard leather drill a 3mm hole every inch along the length having started ¼in from the end.

Thread two needles onto each end of a piece of heavy duty whipping twine that is 8 times the length of the seam. The start is a bit awkward as the leather is slippery on the varnish, nothing is tight and there is an excess of thread. Hold the leather in place with a piece of string for a moment if need be. Coming up from underneath, do two turns to join the first two holes together, with the needles appearing up through the holes

37.1: Leather marking tools

37.3: Planing the edges and soaking the leather

37.2: Measuring the leather width

on completion of the second turn.

Each needle will then go up the seam in a Z pattern which gives an X thread pattern on the seam. The horizontal part of the Z is underneath the seam and the more vertical part on top of the seam. Go up say six holes with the left hand needle then catch up with the right hand needle. You must be careful not to catch the thread of the opposite needle when catching up as if the thread is sewn through the seam cannot be tightened up.

After getting both needles to say the sixth hole, take a small flat head screw driver and starting at the first double sewn hole begin to tighten up the thread. This is a cumulative process so there is no need to have it super tight to the sixth hole at this stage. Go on another say six holes and tighten through again. Don't break the thread otherwise you will have to start again. Make sure the seam is straight down the oar or spar; it is easy for the seam to start peeling off one way.

37.4: Marking out yard leather

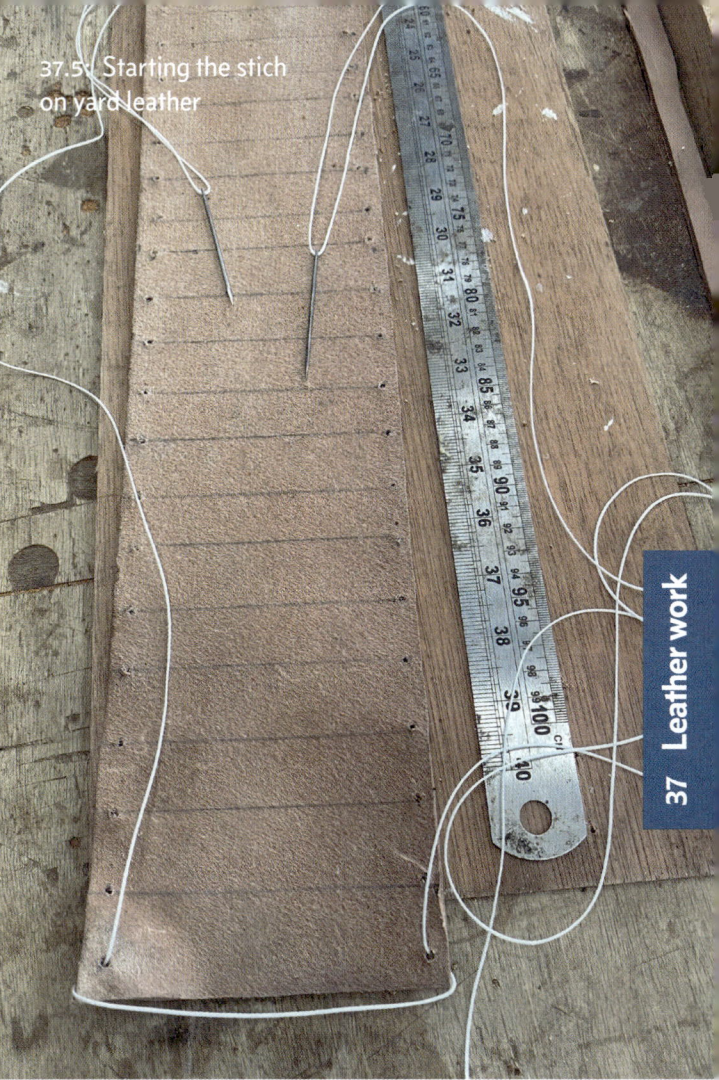

37.5: Starting the stich on yard leather

Once you have got to the end of the seam double sew straight across the last hole as the first hole and then give each end two half hitches around the pair of twines on the surface. These half hitches should pull one by one down into the hole and be all but invisible.

The leather will dry and tighten onto the spar. Give the work a rub with a round wooden pole (a hammer handle works well) and this will smooth ridges out. A copper tack can be put through the two twine holes at either end to secure the leather although this is not strictly necessary.

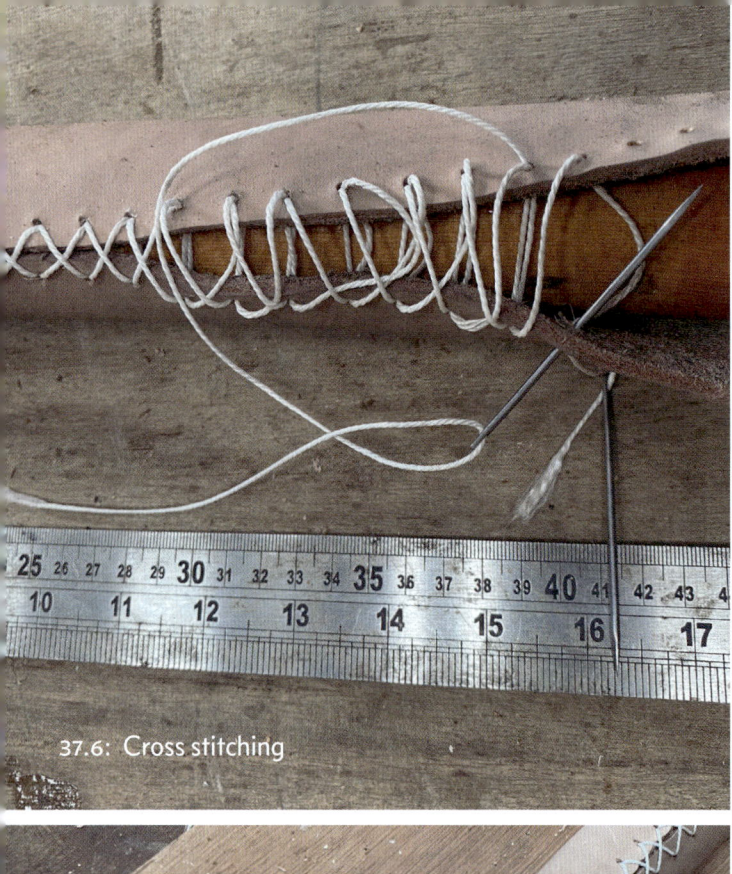

37.6: Cross stitching

37.7: Tightening the twine

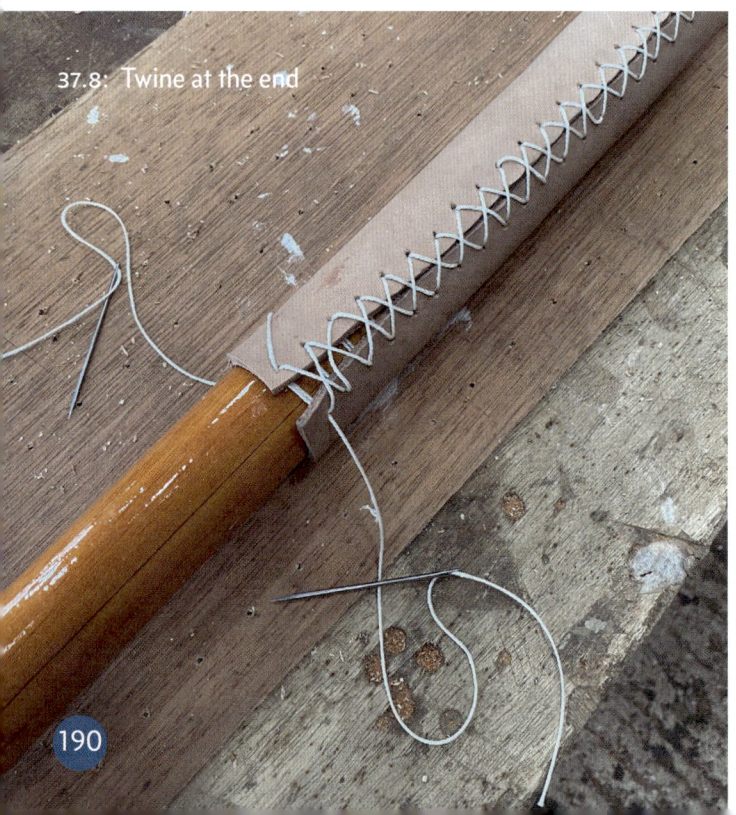

37.8: Twine at the end

37.9: Leathered oars

Comprehensive dinghy plans in various sizes are available from
stirlingandson.co.uk

Published 2021 by
Lodestar Books
71 Boveney Road, London, SE23 3NL, United Kingdom
lodestarbooks.com

Text & photographs copyright © W. N. C. Stirling 2021
The right of W. N. C. Stirling to be identified as the author
of this work has been asserted by him in accordance with the
Copyright, Designs and Patents Act 1988

A CIP catalogue record for this book is available from the British Library
ISBN 978-1-907206-21-4 (sewn edition)
A spiral bound workshop edition is available from the publisher

Typeset by Lodestar Books in Equity and Concourse
Printed in Wales by Gomer Press
All papers used by Lodestar Books are sourced responsibly